How We Got the Bible

Zondervan Quick-Reference Library

ZONDERVAN
QUICK
REFERENCE
LIBRARY

How We Got the Bible

John H. Sailhamer

ZondervanPublishingHouse

Grand Rapids, Michigan

A Division of HarperCollinsPublishers

How We Got the Bible
Copyright © 1998 by John H. Sailhamer

Requests for information should be addressed to:

🏭 ZondervanPublishingHouse
Grand Rapids, Michigan 49530

Library of Congress Cataloging-in-Publication Data

Sailhamer, John.
    How we got the Bible / John H. Sailhamer.
        p. cm. — (Zondervan quick-reference library)
    ISBN: 0-310-20391-0 (pbk.)
    1. Bible—History. I. Title. II. Series.
BS445.S25 1998
220.6-dc 21   97-39134
                                                              CIP

Interior design by Sue Vandenberg Koppenol

Printed in the United States of America

98 99 00 01 02 03 04 /❖ DC/ 10 9 8 7 6 5 4 3 2 1

Contents

Abbreviations of the Books of the Bible

Genesis	Gen.	Nahum	Nah.
Exodus	Ex.	Habakkuk	Hab.
Leviticus	Lev.	Zephaniah	Zeph.
Numbers	Num.	Haggai	Hag.
Deuteronomy	Deut.	Zechariah	Zech.
Joshua	Josh.	Malachi	Mal.
Judges	Judg.	Matthew	Matt.
Ruth	Ruth	Mark	Mark
1 Samuel	1 Sam.	Luke	Luke
2 Samuel	2 Sam.	John	John
1 Kings	1 Kings	Acts	Acts
2 Kings	2 Kings	Romans	Rom.
1 Chronicles	1 Chron.	1 Corinthians	1 Cor.
2 Chronicles	2 Chron.	2 Corinthians	2 Cor.
Ezra	Ezra	Galatians	Gal.
Nehemiah	Neh.	Ephesians	Eph.
Esther	Est.	Philippians	Phil.
Job	Job	Colossians	Col.
Psalms	Ps(s).	1 Thessalonians	1 Thess.
Proverbs	Prov.	2 Thessalonians	2 Thess.
Ecclesiastes	Eccl.	1 Timothy	1 Tim.
Song of Songs	Song	2 Timothy	2 Tim.
Isaiah	Isa.	Titus	Titus
Jeremiah	Jer.	Philemon	Philem.
Lamentations	Lam.	Hebrews	Heb.
Ezekiel	Ezek.	James	James
Daniel	Dan.	1 Peter	1 Peter
Hosea	Hos.	2 Peter	2 Peter
Joel	Joel	1 John	1 John
Amos	Amos	2 John	2 John
Obadiah	Obad.	3 John	3 John
Jonah	Jonah	Jude	Jude
Micah	Mic.	Revelation	Rev.

Introduction

What Is the Bible?

The Bible is one book made up of many books. These were written over many centuries by authors with vastly different backgrounds and cultures. Many authors are well known: Moses, David, Solomon, Ezra, Paul. Such men are not only the leading characters in the Bible, they are also its leading producers. A surprisingly large number of the biblical authors, however, are nameless. Who wrote 1 and 2 Kings, for example, or the book of Hebrews?

Fortunately, the answer to questions of this nature is of no major consequence in understanding the Bible. Who doesn't know and appreciate an old Hollywood movie from the 30s and 40s? Yet how many know about Irving Thalberg of MGM or Jack Warner of Warner Brothers Studios? These were the men who made or produced the movies; they were the "authors" of those films. But we know the movies by watching them, not by learning about their authors and producers. Similarly, we know the Bible and the books of the Bible by reading them.

Some kinds of books (e.g., a diary) require some information about its author before it can be properly understood. Other books, like works of literature and history, are written so that you don't have to know the author to understand and appreciate them. What you need to know is given to you as you read the text. The Bible is that way: It is written simply to be read.

This may sound obvious, but many biblical scholars disagree. The Bible is often approached today as a book so different from other books and so distant from our world that we need to learn all about its world before we can understand what it says. Though there is some merit to that process, it ignores the fact that the Bible was written with a general audience in mind. Their authors were sensitive to the limitations of time and culture that future readers might encounter. They thus took these limitations into consideration when they wrote their books.

If there was a particular historical or cultural item they felt needed explanation, they did so (see 1 Sam. 9:9). What they didn't feel needed explaining was general knowledge (like what the moon is) or unimportant items (like the color of Sarah's eyes). For the most part, they allow the readers to fill in the blanks of their stories. We, of course, often fall back on popular conceptualizations. But whether Moses looks like Charlton Heston in DeMille's *The Ten Commandments* or Michelangelo's Moses does not affect our understanding of Exodus.

The Canon of Scripture

It is one thing to talk about the Bible in general terms, but just exactly what Bible are we talking about? Isn't there some disagreement on what books are even in the Bible? The answer, of course, is that there is disagreement, but not as much as one might think. The standard for what books are in the Bible and what books are not is called the *canon*.

For the Old Testament, the standard was determined long before the birth of Jesus. We have little direct knowledge of the process that brought this about, but we can say with certainty that the Old Testament we have today is the same Scriptures that Jesus used. It was the accepted standard of the Jews in the first century.

In some parts of the church, in the early centuries A.D., additional books were put alongside the canon of the Old Testament in some manuscripts of the Bible. These were popular works that were used in worship and devotion. Later on some of these works were accepted as part of the canon by the Roman Catholic Church and some Orthodox Churches, though not having the same authority as the Bible. These books (up to eighteen) are called the Apocrypha.

There is no dispute about the canon of the New Testament. At an early stage in the history of the church, the New Testament canon was closed, and no new books were added.

The basis for including a book in the canon of the Old and New Testament was twofold: (1) universal acceptance among God's people—Israel for the Old Testament and the church for the New Testament; (2) internal witness of the Holy Spirit—the Spirit of God bore witness to the early readers of Scripture that these books and no others were the inspired Word of God.

How do we know the early church accepted the right books and genuinely witnessed the Spirit's confirmation? For the Old Testament we have the confirmation of Jesus. Throughout his ministry, Jesus quoted and used the Scriptures as God's Word. To accept his authority is to accept the authority of the Old Testament. For the New Testament we have the confirmation of the apostles—the authoritative men who had received direct instruction from Jesus during his earthly ministry. Their acceptance and confirmation of the canon of the New Testament assures us of its authority in our lives today.

The Old Testament and the New Testament

The first half of the Christian Bible, the Old Testament, is also the Bible of Judaism. In Judaism it is simply called the "Hebrew Bible." Christianity shares the Old Testament with that religion because Jesus was a Jew and because he saw the whole of his life as a fulfillment of the ancient Jewish prophets' hope in the coming Messiah. Christians believe that Jesus was the Messiah long expected by the Old Testament prophets. The Old Testament is thus the basis of the New. Without it the New Testament has little meaning.

To speak of an "Old" Testament obviously acknowledges the existence of a "New" Testament. Unfortunately, calling it the "Old" Testament also implies it has been superseded or replaced by the New Testament. That is not the case. The New Testament itself, and the Christian church, acknowledges the full authority of the Old Testament for the life of the Christian. By means of these Old Testament Scriptures, says Paul, the Christian "may be thoroughly equipped for every good work" (2 Tim. 3:17).

The New Testament is the authoritative collection of early Christian writings. Its twenty-seven books are unique in that they, like the Old Testament, are inspired by God (God-breathed). The Old and New Testaments together form the norm of Christian faith and practice. The New Testament was written by the disciples of Jesus, the apostles, and its main teaching is that the Old Testament promise of the "new covenant [or testament]" (Jer. 31:31) was fulfilled in the death and resurrection of Jesus (Luke 22:20; 2 Cor. 3:6).

The Old Testament contains three main parts, as we shall see: the Pentateuch (or the first five books of the Bible, sometimes called the Law or the Torah); the Prophets (the Earlier Prophets are the historical books from Joshua to 2 Kings [excluding Ruth], and the latter prophets are Isaiah, Jeremiah, Ezekiel, and the twelve minor prophets); and the Writings (all the remaining books of the Old Testament, most of which are in the form of poetry). The New Testament contains four main parts. The first four books (the Gospels) give four different perspectives on the life, ministry, death, and resurrection of Jesus; the next book (Acts) outlines the history of the apostolic church; the next twenty-one books are letters written by the apostles to churches and individuals, trying to encourage them in their Christian faith; and the final book is Revelation, a book that describes in apocalyptic language the events of the end times.

The History of the Biblical Text

Old Testment
1. Pentateuch (Law /torah
    first 5 books

2. Prophets
    Earlier (Joshua to 2 Kings excluding Ruth
    Later (Isaiah, Jeremiah, Ezekiel
                and 12 minor prophets
3. Writings (remaining books in form of poetry

New Testiment
1. Gospels
2. Acts (history of apostolic church)
3. Next 21 books are letters written by apostles
    to churches & individuals for encouragement in
    Christian faith
4. Revelation - apocalyptic language
    events of end times

Traditional Account of the History of the Biblical Text

Before we look more closely at the history of the Old and New Testament, we should give that history as it has been traditionally told, and then update and correct that account. Much new information about that history supports the traditional view, though some of it does not.

The traditional view begins with the "autographs," that is, the "original" books of the Bible written by men inspired by the Spirit of God. The first book, the Law (or the Pentateuch), was written by Moses. According to Deuteronomy 31:24ff., the Law was placed in the ark of the covenant. To this first book were added all the succeeding inspired texts as they were written. For example, Joshua wrote the book of Joshua (Josh. 24:26); Samuel wrote Judges, Ruth, and the first part of Samuel; Job wrote his book. Therefore, preserved in the sacred ark was the nascent canon of the Old Testament up to the time of David. During and after the time of Solomon, these books were no longer kept in the ark (cf. 1 Kings 8:6, 9), but rather in the treasury of the temple, where they were cared for by the priests (2 Kings 22:8). More things were added during the time of Hezekiah, such as David's hymns, the proverbs of Solomon, and the prophecies of Isaiah, Hosea, and Micah (cf. Prov. 25:1).

With the destruction of Jerusalem and the Exile in the sixth century, the "autographs" were destroyed, lost, or hopelessly scattered. After the return from exile, Ezra and the "men of the great synagogue," an official board of religious leaders in Israel, collected what remained of the "originals" or corrected the available copies, and, after adding such books as Ezra, Nehemiah, Chronicles, and the prophets Haggai, Zechariah, and Malachi, arranged them into "one systematic corpus." The final canon of the Old Testament was then stored in an ark constructed for the second temple. What we now have as the Hebrew Bible, namely, the Masoretic Text, is a virtual copy of that "autograph." Throughout the centuries, copies of the Masoretic Text were preserved from serious error by divine providence. There were, of course, obscurities and defects in copies of the text that have come down to us, but such features did not inhibit using the text as the final authority in questions of religion and theology.

As far as the New Testament is concerned, its composition and collection followed much the same process as the Old Testament. It was watched over by the apostles in the early church, who wrote some of the books and supervised the writing of others. The many Greek manuscripts of the New Testament that are available enable us to come close to what the original text was.

A General History of the Bible

Our English Bibles are the end product of a long and fascinating process of preservation. The Old Testament was written in Hebrew, the language of ancient and modern Israel; the New Testament in Greek, the common language of the world at the time of Christ.

The general history of the Bible can be divided into three segments: *composition* (when the individual books were written), *canonization* (when the books were collected and arranged into the Bible as a whole, and *consolidation* (when the Bible became an essential part of the Jewish and Christian communities). Both Old and New Testament went through a similar process, though at different times.

For the Old Testament, these periods were separated by two major events: the destruction of Jerusalem and the temple by the Babylonians (586 B.C.) and the destruction of Jerusalem and the temple by the Romans in A.D. 70. Both events had a devastating effect on the religious life of Israel. Prior to each event, the Israelite people were united around their common faith that God was present in their midst both in Scripture and in the temple in Jerusalem, the chosen city where the Messiah would reign. With the destruction of Jerusalem and the temple, however, Israel's identity and faith in God's presence focused exclusively on Scripture.

Three Periods in the History of the Old Testament

Composition	E X I L E	Canon	E X I L E	Consolidation
	586 BC		AD 70	

Most of the New Testament books were written before the destruction of the temple by the Romans in A.D. 70. As Acts shows, the church during its early formative years had close ties with Judaism. The change in Judaism after the destruction of the temple meant also a change for early Christianity. The second major event was the persecution of Christians and subsequent acceptance of Christianity by the Roman empire.

Composition of the Bible

The composition of the books of the Bible covers a large span of time. For the Old Testament it begins with Moses. The core of what is now the Pentateuch was written by Moses. He kept records and wrote down the laws that God revealed at Mount Sinai (see Ex. 17:14, where God commands Moses to write down an account of Israel's battle with the Amalekites; see also Num. 33:2). According to Deuteronomy 31:24, Moses wrote the entire book of Deuteronomy up to that point. As Joshua 1:8 suggests, Moses wrote the first five books as a guide for all future generations to read and meditate on in order to find God's will for their lives.

Scripture also indicates that other books and records were available to the authors of Scripture during the period of composition. A written source called "The Book of Jashar" is mentioned twice (Josh. 10:13; 2 Sam. 1:18); "The Book of the Wars of the LORD" (Num. 21:14), once. The words of the prophets were also put in writing (Jer. 36:2) and thus became available to later biblical writers. In many cases, the prophets themselves no doubt played a major role in the writing of their books (see 36:4). Those who penned the historical books repeatedly refer to the sources they used (such as "the annals of the kings"). We should thus think of the composition of the books of the Bible as a process much like a modern documentary film. Authentic archival records of the past are preserved in a meaningful way by collecting and arranging them into a complete picture. By means of added narration and music, documentary films maintain an even continuity and general thematic structure.

In many cases, the books of the Old Testament went through more than one edition. The death of Moses, for example, was added to the end of the Pentateuch (Deut. 34:5–12). An earlier conclusion to a collection of Davidic psalms is found at the end of Psalm 72. The composition of the Old Testament was thus accomplished in stages. Earlier editions were updated and reissued for later generations, just as documentary films are today.

The composition of the New Testament is much the same as the Old Testament. In the case of the Gospels, Acts, and Revelation, the writers of the New Testament may have emulated the writers of the Old Testament. The Gospel writers (including Acts) relied heavily on eyewitness accounts and records of the life of Jesus (cf. Luke 1:1–4). The New Testament letters are, as they claim, actual letters written to specific churches and individuals.

The Shaping of the Canon

How were the books of the Old Testament and New Testament gathered and shaped into the completed versions of the Bible we now possess? That process apparently took place in several stages. We must first acknowledge that we have no surviving eyewitness accounts of the process. There are later accounts, but their exact meaning is unclear; in most cases, they are too far removed from the process itself to be of real value. All we have to go on are the traces of the formation of the canon within the Scriptures themselves. We can discover in these texts the work of those who arranged and shaped it, just as a modern geologist surveys the earth and finds traces of the processes that brought about the shape of its surface today.

The basic structure of the Old Testament canon is different in the Hebrew text than in our English editions. In the English Bible the Old Testament is arranged according to literary type. The historical books, for example, are placed together, as are the poetic and prophetic books. This order follows that of the ancient Greek and Latin translations. It was not until the Reformation that a renewed interest arose in the Hebrew Bible.

In the Hebrew Bible, the books are arranged according to their content and central themes (we will say more below about the meaning behind this different order). Note the difference in the order of the books in the Hebrew Old Testament:

(1) The Law (Pentateuch). Genesis, Exodus, Leviticus, Numbers, Deuteronomy
(2) The Prophets. Former: Joshua, Judges, Samuel, Kings
    Latter: Isaiah, Jeremiah, Ezekiel, Twelve Minor Prophets
(3) The Writings. Psalms, Job, Proverbs, Ruth, Song of
    Songs, Ecclesiastes, Lamentations, Esther, Daniel, Ezra,
    Nehemiah, Chronicles

The chief difference from our Bible lies in the location of the prophetic books, the poetic books, and the later historical books (Ezra, Nehemiah, and Chronicles). Daniel is not included among the prophets, and Ruth is not in with the historical books.

The order of the New Testament books follows a similar threefold pattern.

(1) The Gospels. Matthew, Mark, Luke, John
(2) The History of the Church. Acts
(3) The Apostolic Writings. Remaining books of the New Testament

This official order of the New Testament canon was established sometime before the middle of the fourth century.

The Consolidation of the Bible

The closing of the biblical canon did not mean the end of the development of the Bible. Both the Old Testament and the New Testament underwent considerable development during the early centuries of the church, when the communities primarily responsible for preserving the text were themselves taking shape from and giving shape to the Bible. This was a time of consolidation.

In the case of the Old Testament, the period of consolidation occurred during the time when the Christian church and Judaism were parting ways. These two communities had fundamentally different ideas about the meaning of these Scriptures and openly debated those differences. For the most part, after the second century, the Christian church was content to leave the Hebrew Bible in the hands of the Jews. True, Christian scholars such as Jerome busied themselves with the Hebrew text and tried to perfect and popularize existing Old Testament translations for use in the church. But once that work was accomplished, the church felt comfortable for over a millennium with its Greek and Latin translations.

In the meantime, skilled and dedicated Jewish scholars undertook the task of consolidating the Hebrew Bible. When the church returned to the Hebrew Bible in the Reformation, it had become a part of the Jewish traditional literature. In many ways, it was not the same document that the church had abandoned. In a passage such as 2 Samuel 23:1, for example, where in New Testament times there had been a reference to the Messiah, now in the Hebrew text was only a reference to David.

The New Testament also went through a period of consolidation, similar to the Hebrew Bible, only within the confines of the Christian church. Its text was adjusted to the community responsible for its preservation. By comparing manuscripts from the earliest centuries of the church with those of the medieval period, we can tell how the church altered the text according to its theological dictates. For example, a passage such as 1 John 5:7–8, "For these are three that testify: the Spirit, the water and the blood," was transformed into a Trinitarian formula: "For there are three what testify in heaven: the Father, the Word and the Holy Spirit, and these three are one." Throughout this process, the Bible was preserved intact but not unscathed. The task of textual criticism, the science of texts, is to restore the Bible to its original state.

Textual Criticism

Textual criticism is the science of ancient texts. *Biblical* textual criticism is devoted specifically to preserving and restoring the original texts of Scripture. Ancient texts can be restored just like antique furniture and classic automobiles. Figuratively speaking, a lot of paint and varnish has to be stripped off in order to find the original. Just as we can learn a lot about the previous owner of an old car when we restore it, so we can learn a lot about the early communities who used these ancient manuscripts.

The subject matter that textual criticism uses is ancient manuscripts (a *manuscript* is a handwritten document). There are thousands of Hebrew and Greek manuscripts of the Bible or parts of it. There are also thousands of copies of translations of the Bible. After the invention of the printing press, there was, for the most part, little further use of handwritten texts.

A manuscript is rarely copied exactly as it is written, and so minor variations creep into the text. In the ancient world, however, being a scribe was a noble profession, and most scribes took great pride in their work. They made comparably few errors in copying. But sometimes in copying texts as revered as the Bible, scribes felt compelled to add a word here and there to clarify or even, if they believed there was a problem, to correct the text. Sometimes they omitted parts of the text, either because they accidentally overlooked it or because they felt it did not belong. Over the years the manuscripts have probably suffered more from well-meaning scribes than from careless ones.

Fortunately, there are enough manuscripts of the Bible that we can usually spot a correction or clarification. The task of textual criticism is to locate and "weed out" such scribal alterations to the original text. This method of criticism is important in reconstructing the history of the Bible, since the Bible itself tells us little about its own history.

Recent years have seen many discoveries of ancient manuscripts of the Bible. The most notable have been the Dead Sea Scrolls—manuscripts stored in caves near the Dead Sea since the time of Christ. Most of these were manuscripts of the Hebrew Bible. They take us back to the time before the consolidation of the Bible within the Jewish and Christian communities. They thus give us a glimpse of the state of the Bible at the time the New Testament was written.

The "Original Text"

One of the most difficult concepts used in the study of the Bible's history is the notion of the "original text." One might think it would be easy to define the notion of an "original text." In one sense it is. The original text is that manuscript written by the author of a book of the Bible. The problem, however, is that for many today, "original text" does not mean the author's text. There are, in fact, at least three different viewpoints regarding this.

(1) For some, particularly the theologians of the seventeenth and eighteenth centuries, the "original text" was not the author's own text but the accurate copies of his text that they had in manuscript form. They were well aware that they did not have the actual pieces of parchment that the original authors of Scripture used. Because they believed the "original texts" were inspired, those same theologians were troubled by that fact. What good is an inspired text if we do not have it? Their solution was to call the copies of the texts that we have the "original texts" and the historical author's texts the "autographa" (a Greek word meaning "his own written text"). Thus they could say that we have the "original texts" of Scripture and yet not mean that we have the author's own manuscripts. But there was a major flaw in their thinking, which became evident in the latter part of the eighteenth century. The "copies" that they had called the "original texts" and considered to be exact copies of the autographa were not as accurate as they had supposed. When scholars began comparing manuscripts, they found many variations in the manuscripts. This discovery led to a redefinition of the term "original text."

(2) In the nineteenth century, "original text" came to mean the actual manuscript written by the hand of an author of Scripture. In other words, the original texts were those manuscripts that we no longer have in our possession, since they have long since disappeared. Many still understand the term "original text" in that sense.

(3) Finally, many understand "original text" to be that form of the text that we can restore and locate at a particular time and place in history by textual criticism. We can, for example, speak of the "original text" that Jesus used in the first century. We can even reconstruct that text. We can also speak of the "original text" that Ezra used, though that text would be harder to reconstruct.

Consequently, whenever we use the phrase "original text," we must be careful to define it so as to eliminate confusion.

The Masoretic Text of the Old Testament

The Masoretic text, the traditional version of the Hebrew Bible, is the form of the Scriptures found in medieval Jewish manuscripts. The word "Masoretic," in fact, means "traditional." It is the form of the Hebrew Bible used in Jewish literature and worship, and it is meticulously exact. Every letter, vowel, and accent has been carefully preserved as it has been handed down by tradition. Orthodox Jews consider this text to be an exact copy of the "autographs." Christian scholarship of the sixteenth and seventeenth centuries were heavily influenced by this view and also believed that the Masoretic text was virtually an exact replica of what God had inspired the authors of the Bible to write.

The Masoretic text consists of three parts: the Hebrew consonants, the signs for the vowels, and the accents. The Hebrew language was usually written without vowels. Early manuscripts of the Bible were thus written only with consonants. One had to know the vowels of a particular word in order to read the text. Large sections of the Bible were committed to memory by those who read the Bible. Reading it was similar to singing familiar hymns in church. Most people already know the songs by heart. They look at the hymnbook simply to jog their memory. The Jews of old knew much of the Bible by heart and looked at the text as a guide to memory.

In time, however, certain scribes began marking in the vowels, using a system of dots and dashes added above and below the Hebrew consonants. The scribes who recorded the vowels in the manuscripts were called Masoretes, because they preserved the Masorah ("tradition"). Along with the vowels, these Masoretes also added accents to each word, to ensure proper intonation for each word and proper punctuation.

By supplying each word of the Bible with a specific set of vowels and accents, the Masoretes contributed greatly to standardizing the traditional meaning of each biblical text. Much of the meaning of the Hebrew text is linked to the specific vowels given to the words. There is no evidence that the Masoretes changed the text in any way, either in the consonants or the vowels. They preserved the version of the Bible handed down to them by tradition. Since they began their work sometime after the fourth and fifth centuries, the Masoretes managed only to preserve the tradition from that period. By that time, however, the "traditional" understanding of the Old Testament had varied considerably from other earlier texts.

Pre-Masoretic and Proto-Masoretic Texts

The "pre-Masoretic" period was a formative and defining moment for the Hebrew Bible. During this time, there was no unanimity about the meaning of the Old Testament. There was, in fact, much debate about its meaning, particularly those passages that the church and the New Testament had related to Jesus.

By the time the Masoretes began preserving the traditional interpretation of the Hebrew Bible, the Jewish-Christian debates had ceased; both groups had gone their separate ways. But early in those debates, most Christians had chosen to read the Old Testament in Greek or Latin translations, the language spoken by the majority of them. These Christians knew that many of their most important arguments could be better sustained from the translations than from the Hebrew Bible itself. The Hebrew Bible was thus left in the hands of its Jewish custodians.

Those primarily responsible for preserving the traditional interpretation of the Scriptures in Judaism were the "scribes." Before the time of the Masoretes, much scholarly activity had already been expended on the Hebrew text so that it conformed to the traditional meaning. This does not mean the scribes altered the Hebrew text; rather, even before the first century, various versions of the Hebrew Bible were already in circulation. Some manuscripts resembled the version now preserved in the Masoretic Text (those are called the "proto-Masoretic" texts). Others resembled the versions of the Hebrew Bible reflected in the Greek and Latin translations. They were essentially "non-Masoretic" in nature. The scribes who consolidated the Hebrew Bible within Judaism chose those biblical texts that were essentially "proto-Masoretic."

The "non-Masoretic" texts thus fell by the wayside. What remains of them today is known from recently discovered manuscripts from the Dead Sea Scrolls and from ancient Greek and Latin translations. It also appears that Jesus and the New Testament writers relied heavily on these "non-Masoretic" texts.

Pre-Masoretic Period	Masoretic Period
Proto-Masoretic Text Non-Masoretic Text(s)	Masoretic Text

What are the implications from this early history of the Hebrew Bible? (1) The Masoretic text is an extremely well-preserved version of the Hebrew Bible, but not the only version. (2) Much in the Masoretic text comes from the formative period in rabbinic Judaism and is not related to the meaning of the Old Testament during the time of Christ. (3) The other early versions of the Hebrew Bible that come to us through the manuscripts from the Dead Sea and the Greek and Latin translations are valuable sources for determining the original text.

The Majority Text of the New Testament

The early medieval period (A.D. 600–1000) was a crucial time for the history of the Bible. At the same time as the Hebrew Bible was receiving its definitive form within Judaism by the Masoretes, the Greek New Testament text was receiving its definitive form within Christianity. The center of Christianity at this time was the Greek-speaking Byzantine empire. Christianity was the official religion of the empire, and great pains were taken to ensure uniformity of doctrine and practice. As a result, the manuscript copies of the Greek New Testament from this period show remarkable uniformity. These manuscripts are called the "Majority Text."

As with the Hebrew Masoretic text, the Greek Majority Text was virtually the only form of the New Testament known to the church throughout most of its history. It was thus natural that it be identified as the "original text." After the invention of the printing press in the fifteenth century, printed editions of the New Testament used manuscripts that represented the Majority Text. It thus became the basis of most early English translations, such as the King James Version.

All that changed in the nineteenth century. As new manuscript discoveries were made, scholars realized there were earlier and, in many cases, better versions of the Greek New Testament, which differed markedly from the Majority Text. It thus became apparent that long before the text was standardized in the Byzantium empire, great care had been taken in other parts of the world to preserve the Greek Bible. Egypt, for example, had a large Christian community in the early centuries of the church. Many of their New Testament Greek manuscripts, copied on paper made from the papyrus plant, have survived because of extreme arid conditions. The New Testament was also copied onto large leather pages and bound into books. Such books, or "codices," have lasted over fifteen hundred years.

Both the codices and papyri have preserved versions of the New Testament from the earliest centuries. This has given New Testament textual criticism much more to work with in restoring the "original text" of the New Testament. Virtually all modern editions of the Greek New Testament are based on manuscripts that reflect the form of the New Testament in the early second century; these editions have become the basis of most modern English translations.

But because the King James Version was so popular and its phraseology so much a part of the hymns and devotional literature of the church,

efforts to revise it were met with stiff resistance. And since modern trans-
lations do not rely on the Majority Text, the average layperson wonders:
Doesn't it make more sense to use the most common version of the Greek
New Testament? Doesn't that more likely reflect God's providence?

God's Providence and the History of the Bible (1)

A central question must be raised in the study of the history of the Bible. For both Old and New Testaments we have seen that the most commonly used manuscripts of the Bible have, for the most part, not reflected the original text. Whether the church used the Greek and Latin translations of the Old Testament (first 1500 years) or the Hebrew Masoretic text, neither approach gave it a version of the Old Testament that actually reflected the earliest version. For nearly the same amount of time, the church used copies of the Greek New Testament that were, in many places, more in line with later church doctrine than representative of the original Greek text; no wonder theologians argued for the Majority Text.

During the seventeenth century, most orthodox Protestant theologians argued that God had providentially preserved the original text in the form of the Masoretic text. They insisted that each and every detail of this text had been penned by Moses and the prophets. Though they acknowledged that no single manuscript could claim to be a precise copy of the "autographs," they insisted that the Masoretic text, with vowel points and accents, were exact, if imperfect, replicas of the "autographs." In these arguments, the Reformers were arguing against the church's dependence on tradition. A major part of that tradition was reflected in the Latin translation of the Bible used by the church (the Vulgate). The Reformers insisted that the church should go back to the original Hebrew text and no longer base its theology and practice on the Latin. Many church doctrines the Reformers objected to were, in fact, supported by the Vulgate.

The Roman Catholic Church was quick to respond. They charged that the Hebrew Bible had been changed at key points by the Jews who copied it, so that the Masoretic text could not be trusted. They argued that the true version of the Old Testament was the Vulgate, which had been translated, they maintained, before the Hebrew text had been changed. The Protestant theologians responded by insisting that the Masoretic Text was the original text. Their argument consisted of two central points. (1) Since no other Hebrew manuscripts were known to them except the Masoretic text, the main issue was whether the church should use Hebrew or Latin texts of the Old Testament. Since God had spoken to the authors in Hebrew, the church should use the Hebrew. (2) God, in his governance and providential care for the church, would not allow his inspired Word, the Bible, to suffer loss or injury. Therefore, the text they had in hand—the Masoretic Old Testament—was the best possible version of the "autographs."

God's Providence and the History of the Bible (2)

The church in the seventeenth and eighteenth centuries used the same argument from divine providence for its defense of the Majority Text of the New Testament as it did for the Masoretic text. Theologians claimed that Majority Text of the New Testament must be the best text because it is the one God preserved for use in the church. Would God preserve an inferior text? This argument did, in fact, hold for most in the church as long as there was no substantial evidence to the contrary.

When such evidence began to emerge, however, the church's defense of the traditional texts of the Old and New Testament began to dwindle. Evidence to the contrary came in three forms. (1) Increasing study of the Masoretic text produced massive evidence that many of its features were innovations by the Masoretes. Though many brilliant biblical scholars continued to insist that every detail of the Masoretic text had been preserved from the biblical authors themselves, the evidence to the contrary became overwhelming. By the beginning of the eighteenth century, the argument for God's providential care of a supposed original Masoretic text had been abandoned. Ironically, the modern discovery of the Dead Sea Scrolls would have helped those biblical scholars had they known of it. Moreover, their argument could have been more easily sustained had they not taken an all-or-nothing position.

(2) Ancient manuscripts of the Bible began to be collected and compared. For the Old Testament, these showed that the agreement between the various Masoretic Texts was not nearly as uniform as had been assumed. There were many minor differences among various copies. Though such evidence was not a frontal assault on the argument from divine providence, it did weaken it considerably. It became obvious that divine providence had not intended to keep the church's Bible absolutely free from changes. While no one disputed that God had providentially protected his Word through the ages, clearly the Masoretic text and Majority Text were only one means of his doing that.

(3) Archaeologists and researchers began to uncover new and earlier manuscripts of the Bible. As long as biblical scholars had no other texts by which to measure the accuracy of the Masoretic text and Majority Text, it was easy to say they were "pure." But as soon as they discovered other texts of the Old and New Testament that differed from the traditional ones, it became clear that God's providence was not necessarily on the side of the traditional texts. Once new texts were discovered, it could just as easily be argued that God's providence had led to the discovery of those new texts to correct what had been used until then.

The Hebrew Old Testament

Writing

The Hebrew language is at least four thousand years old. The language itself is that of the people who lived along the western seaboard and inland foothills of ancient Syria and Canaan. Scientifically, ancient Hebrew is classified as a Canaanite language. As a written language, its alphabet consisted of consonants only, though when it was pronounced, it contained vowel sounds. We know that because when ancient Canaanite scribes wrote some of their words, such as names, in other alphabets, they used vowels, and we are able to see how the words were pronounced. This consonantal feature had far-reaching consequences for the history of the Bible.

Even though the vowels of a Hebrew word were not written, they are essential to its meaning. Without them, the consonants are capable of a wide range of meanings. The consonants אדם, for example, can mean "red," "man," or "I will be silent." Only the vowels show the difference. When a Hebrew text was written without its vowels, it was assumed that anyone reading that passage knew the correct vowels.

In order for the ancients to read the Old Testament accurately, they had to know what vowels to supply each word. Usually the context was of some help, but the only sure way to know the proper vowels was to have the text memorized; the written text with its consonants then served only as aids to memory. When Jesus picked up the scroll of Isaiah and read from it in Luke 4:17, this act shows he had received a great deal of training in reading the Bible. He must have memorized large portions of the Hebrew Old Testament in order to know what vowels to use.

Over the course of time, the Hebrew scribes began to mark certain vowels within a word, in order to make sure the correct vowels were read along with the consonants they wrote. They used certain letters both as vowels and as consonants. This assured them that future generations would read the words correctly. Any skilled reader was able to distinguish between the use of a specific letter as a consonant or a vowel. For the rest of the word, however, the reader had to be familiar with the proper vowels. The meaning of the Old Testament was preserved in this way for over a thousand years. It was only in the Masoretic period that scribes began to insert every vowel mark into the Hebrew text.

Records

Records were a necessary part of the composition of the Hebrew Old Testament. Much of what we now have in the Old Testament consists of a collection of early records. In one sense, the Hebrew Bible is like a huge scrapbook of newspaper and magazine clippings. To be sure, those clippings have been arranged into a coherent work of literature—but, when put under the microscope, we know that the Bible contains many small, precisely recorded documents.

We, of course, have the Bible as a finished product, and we do not have access to earlier copies or fragments of the original pieces. Some have suggested that those earlier pieces were almost entirely oral, though when stories and bits of information come together in oral form, they tend to merge and lose their distinctive shape. Oral stories and records are more fluid, taking the shape of whatever larger container holds them. But the pieces of which the Bible is made seem to have retained their shape.

Human begins have always felt a need to keep written records. The art of writing was, in fact, a by-product of that need. Some of the earliest written documents we now possess are administrative texts written on clay tablets. Signs that later developed into letters of an alphabet originated as marks made in soft clay to denote the number of a farmer's sheep or the quantity of oil in a clay jar. Early scribes in Canaan invented the alphabet at about the same time as Abraham was making his way into the land of Canaan. That alphabet was the first one of its kind and is the grandfather of all modern alphabets. It consisted of twenty-two letters, all consonants. But with these twenty-two signs, a scribe could record every word in his own language, and potentially at least, every word in every language on earth.

Not only could ancient Hebrew now be used to record information and stories; because of the nature of the alphabet it could be written on virtually any kind of surface with a sharp tool. It did not require a soft clay tablet or a painted surface of a wall. Once the alphabet had been invented, in fact, one of the most common forms of writing surfaces became fragments of broken jars. Such records have lasted for hundreds and thousands of years. A simple scratch on a flat stone can record an event in the life of an ancestor for a hundred generations. Many such small written documents are as readable today as they were more than three thousand years ago.

Book Making

At what point were early written records collected and arranged into book form? The way that question is stated involves a certain kind of anachronism. The English word "book" refers to a bound paper document with pages. Technically, such a work is called a "codex" and is a relatively late development. In the ancient world, a "book" was often little more than a makeshift writing surface, such as a stone or a broken piece of pottery. Sometimes it consisted of a scroll—that is, writing on the surface of a rather long piece of material that was stored by rolling the document onto a round stick and sealing the end together with wax. In the widest sense, however, a "book" was a coherent literary document with a broad scope and a particular purpose.

Moses wrote such a document (Deut. 31:24), which was handed over to Joshua after Moses' death (Josh. 1:8). Joshua was to read that book "day and night" as the source of his strength and trust in God. We can only assume that this book was a sort of first edition of the Pentateuch. But whatever the extent of that book, one thing is certain—the book Moses wrote was the prototype of all subsequent biblical books. It was the one great legacy he passed on to the future generations. He did not, of course, invent the art of writing a lengthy work on papyrus. The Egyptians had done that for centuries before him. It was the book as the embodiment of God's acts and promises made to his people that Moses invented. He was the inventor of "the Bible."

The actual procedure of writing a book in biblical times is described in Jeremiah 36. The Lord tells Jeremiah to take a "scroll" and write on it "all the words I have spoken to you . . . from the time I began speaking to you in the reign of Josiah till now" (Jer. 36:2). This presupposes that Jeremiah had been keeping records of those words. The prophet read the words of these records to Baruch, his scribe (Jer. 36:18). Baruch wrote down the words on a scroll in columns (36:23), and then took the book to its intended audience and read it aloud (36:8–10). He personally had to read it aloud to the scribes because, in all likelihood, it contained no vowels and would not be intelligible without him. After the scribes heard Baruch read the book, they were then able to take it to the king and read it to him (36:21).

Composition

How were the books of the Bible composed? There are at least three approaches offered in answer to this question.

(1) *The critical view.* The viewpoint represented by many modern critics sees the formation of the books of the Bible as a lengthy and complex process. The Bible is essentially a record of what Israel believed about itself, and the individual books are the result of numerous uses and reuses of the same material, plus countless additions. These books arose out of the needs of various Israelite communities. To cope with times of crises or simply to give meaning to everyday life, these communities used the religious stories and traditions that had been passed on to them. Each one understood these stories and traditions as its own and in its own way. As they retold their stories, they changed them to fit their own new situation. The words of one prophet were picked up and attributed to another. The deeds of one patriarch were recast as the deeds of another. The present-day books of the Bible represent the final word on the meaning of Israel's past. According to modern critics, to attempt to unscramble these books in an effort to get back to what actually happened in Israel's ancient past is a hopeless venture.

(2) *The compositional view.* Others see the biblical books as the result of an intentional endeavor to recount what God had accomplished in Israel's past and what he had promised for their future. The authors were like curators of great art museums. They collected the works of past masters, displayed them in frames, and arranged them in appropriate settings in order to enhance all that the works contain. The author of Isaiah, for example, gathered the written words of the prophet and arranged them in a book in the same way as an artist uses colors. Isaiah's words became the words of the author. In reality, the prophet's words speak for themselves within the context provided by the author of the book. A modern analogy might be a radio program that takes the recorded messages of a well-known speaker and edits them into a thirty-minute broadcast. Many features are not a part of the original messages—music, introductions, the voice of a narrator, etc. But the whole broadcast, like the whole biblical book, is intended to disseminate the words of the speaker.

(3) *The common view.* The average layperson views the composition of the biblical books in much the same light as a modern nonfiction book would be written. The author sets out to record what he has seen

as an eyewitness to the events he is recounting. He may use notes or refer to records, but the words of the book are his words.

In our opinion, the compositional view best describes the process of biblical authorship.

The Critical View

The critical view is best represented by the documentary hypothesis. Its classical expression is found in the works of Julius Wellhausen, a nineteenth-century Old Testament scholar. Few biblical scholars today hold to his position in all its details, but in its broad outline, Wellhausen's view still represents modern critical approaches to the Bible.

According to Wellhausen, the Pentateuch is no more a product of a single author than the Grand Canyon is a product of a single landscaper. Just as the Grand Canyon was the result of a long and slow process, one must be prepared to see the Pentateuch as the end result of a long and complicated process. One does not approach the Grand Canyon from the viewpoint of its design or intent, but rather from the viewpoint of its result. That is, the Colorado River did not start out with the intent of creating the Grand Canyon; rather, the Grand Canyon was the result of the courses taken by that river. Similarly, the Pentateuch was not planned the way it now reads. It simply happened, and our task is to retrace the steps that led to its present formation.

Wellhausen sought to retrace the process of the formation of the Pentateuch in much the same way that a geologist studies the formation of the Grand Canyon. He looked for layers of texts that had been deposited by the flow of time and tradition. He believed he had found at least four principal layers. An early version of the Pentateuch was the J-Document. Lying on top of it was a slightly later one, the E-Document. These two documents told essentially the same story of the early patriarchs, their sojourn in Egypt, their escape from there, and their possession of the land of Canaan, but with a slightly different slant. They were fastened together so closely by later editors that it was nearly impossible to separate them. A third layer was called the D-Document, consisting primarily of Deuteronomy and a few supplemental links to the earlier sources. The final layer was the P-Document, the riverbed that gave the Pentateuch its final form.

Because the Pentateuch had been shaped by such a variety of sources, Wellhausen surmised that many inconsistencies must originally have been exposed on the surface. With time, however, these rough edges were trimmed and smoothed. But careful scholars can still detect the many diverse and incongruous strata that lie just beneath that surface.

This is not the place to offer a critique of Wellhausen's view. It was a remarkably creative idea in its day and won the acceptance of many biblical scholars. Like most theories spun in the nineteenth century, however, modern scholarship views this approach as much too simplistic.

The Compositional View

The compositional view provides a viable alternative to the classical documentary hypothesis. It differs from the classical critical view in two important respects. (1) It views the end product of the Pentateuch, for example, in light of the intentional design and purpose of its author. The Pentateuch is not merely the result of a process; rather, the author designed it in a particular way. If we use the analogy of the Grand Canyon again, the compositional view sees the Pentateuch as the "Grand Canyon Ride" at Disneyland. There the entire "Grand Canyon" is the result of a purposeful design. Each turn in the river is planned to correspond to the line of track that winds through it. The trees, rocks, and animals that one sees while riding on the train each have a purpose and contribute to the meaning of the whole.

(2) The compositional view does not assume that earlier versions of the Pentateuch once existed to rival the present edition. There were no earlier J and E documents—at least, not that we can reconstruct. The present edition of the Pentateuch was composed of earlier "pieces" of texts—stories, genealogies, laws, and poems—woven together to form the big picture that the Pentateuch now is. What those earlier "pieces" looked like or where they came from is of no concern. While one may possibly isolate and reconstruct some of the earlier pieces, such an endeavor is not necessary to appreciate the textual strategy in the Pentateuch. In a word, the compositional approach is about strategy, not strata.

The compositional approach starts with the idea that the present form of any biblical book has a literary plan. There is something in store for the reader of the book—much like there is something in store for one who rides the "Grand Canyon Ride." To "get" what the Pentateuch is about, one must read it—just like one must go on the train ride through the "Grand Canyon." It is also possible, however, to peer beneath the surface of the text to get a sense of where the author is leading us. We can retrace his strategy and understand how he accomplished his purpose. Why did he use a poem here and a genealogy there? Why did he repeat a similar story several times in the same book? Why does the Pentateuch begin with an account of creation and conclude with the death of Moses? Yet one does not have to know the answers to these questions to understand the book. Such questions are like asking why a great artist chooses this or that color of paint. We don't need to know the reason in order to appreciate his work of art.

The Common View

When most people read the Bible, they take little thought about how it was put together. And that's how it should be. When we watch a movie, for example, few of us observe the lighting of an indoor scene, watch for different camera angles, or look for the editing techniques. We simply watch the movie and allow those techniques to make it come alive for us. To analyze it requires us to become detached from it. It is the same with reading a good book. So there is no need for us to detach ourselves from the Bible to see how it was put together.

The common view, therefore, simply assumes the Bible was written as any other book. The authors took out their pens and started writing. They may have used notes and quotes, but in the end, the book is all in their own words. Here the common view contrasts with the compositional view. In the compositional view, the Hebrew Bible is sewn together like a quilt. Pieces of cloth from here and there are made into a single bed covering. The common view sees the biblical books more like a bedspread—sewn as one piece.

One of the reasons the common view is, in fact, so common is that most people read the Bible in translations. A translation inevitably makes the text uniform. Whatever rough edges may exist in the Hebrew text are smoothed over in a translation. To continue our analogy, no matter how many pieces are sewed together in a quilt, if you throw a bedspread on top of it, it smooths the quilt out. A translation lays on the Hebrew Bible like a bedspread lays on a quilt.

Does it matter which view one has of the way the Bible was written? In many ways it does not. As we have said, the purpose of reading the Bible is to get its message, and we can get it simply by reading it. In another sense, however, it is important to understand how the Bible was written, for then one can appreciate more precisely the things that are in the Bible. If we can reconstruct the author's overall strategy, we can more clearly understand the relevance or importance of some of the parts. If, for example, an author has used poetic texts in order to highlight the central themes of the book, it makes us more sensitive to what those poems have to say. If an author has used genealogies in a narrative to link key characters in the story, it prompts us to look more carefully at what is said about the characters in a genealogy. In short, it makes us more sensitive and alerts readers to the intricacies of the Bible.

The Composition of an Old Testament Book

We have suggested that the compositional approach leads us to a better understanding of the final shape that the biblical writers have given their books. In that shape lies a textual strategy. The authors have arranged and refined the individual texts into a complete picture. Like any work of art or piece of literature, we must read it carefully and thoughtfully to appreciate the author's meaning. We have to see how the pieces fit together to form the whole.

Let's take the book of Isaiah as an example. This book contains both the written words of Isaiah and a narrative story about him. The former were presumably recorded as Isaiah delivered them, perhaps preserved by him and his disciples (Isa. 8:16). The book's purpose was to present to its readers the prophet's message during some of the darkest days of Israel's apostasy. The author used Isaiah's own words to tell his story. The prophet was called to prophesy when God's people were being sorely oppressed by the cruel and mighty Assyrian empire. In that context he offered not only threats of judgment, but also words of hope. God would send a Redeemer King from the house of David (7:14; 9:6–7) and establish his kingdom (chs. 11–12).

As the author has arranged the material, the reader is left with the impression that the promised Redeemer would come in Isaiah's own day. However, the insertion of the narrative chapters 36–39 into the prophecies of Isaiah suggests otherwise. Those narratives, which speak of the coming Babylonian captivity, show that the prophet's words looked beyond the immediate events in his own life and times, beyond the time of Israel's oppression under Assyria, and beyond the time of their exile into Babylon, to the time of Israel's return from their captivity. Were Isaiah's visions perhaps then to be fulfilled during the days of Israel's return from Babylon, or beyond even those days? As we keep reading, we see that the prophet's visions do indeed point beyond the days of Israel's return from Babylonian captivity, as the insertion of the "servant songs" indicates. The prophet's visions point to the days of the coming Messiah, the Servant of the Lord, who was to suffer for his own people and the nations and who would usher in a time of peace and prosperity (Isa. 53). Ultimately, the visions of Isaiah extend into a future that includes "new heavens and a new earth" (65:17) and an eternal peace for the people of God.

What is true for Isaiah is true for the rest of the books of the Old Testament. Each book is composed with an overriding purpose in mind, reflected in the way in which the material is arranged and shaped.

Redaction

Many books of the Bible (e.g., the Pentateuch) have later additions attached to them. Such additions to a book are called *redactions*. Redaction is different than composition. Composition results in the production of a book; redaction results in an adjustment made to a book. In the forties and fifties, car enthusiasts often bought old cars and modified them ("souped them up"). That was redaction. When Ford Motor Company made the Model T Ford, that was composition. If someone bought a Model T and put in a new engine and dual carburetors, that was redaction.

Two of the most important redactions occur at the end of the Pentateuch (the death of Moses in Deut. 34:5–10) and end of the Prophets (the exhortation to watch for the return of Elijah in Mal. 4:4–6). Both redactions include the same kind of material. The end of Deuteronomy speaks of the coming of a prophet like Moses, who showed "mighty power" and performed "awesome deeds." The end of Malachi speaks of the return of the prophet Elijah, who, as we know from the historical books, did great signs and wonders like Moses. Elijah was a prophet like Moses, and Elijah was coming again! Both passages also stress the importance of the role of Moses in giving Israel the Scriptures.

Moreover, these two redactions, strategically located at the seams of the large sections of the Old Testament canon (the Pentateuch and the Prophets), also correspond to the beginning of the Joshua and the Psalms (the first books of the Prophets and the Writings). Joshua begins by exhorting its readers to meditate day and night on the law of Moses; he who does so will prosper (Josh. 1:8). This is the same exhortation offered at the opening of the book of Psalms (Ps. 1:2–3)—it uses the same words! The following chart shows how in the order of the books in the Hebrew Bible, these passages occur alongside each other.

Shaping of the Hebrew Canon

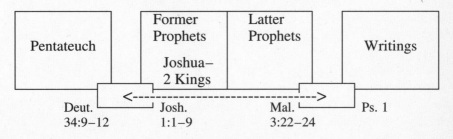

Such convergence of material, so strategically located, suggests the presence of intelligent life in the shaping of the Old Testament canon. It also suggests that someone is trying to tell us something about the meaning of the books of the Hebrew Bible. The additional comments and exhortations have been put at the seams of these sections to guide the readers of Scripture.

The Shaping of the Old Testament Canon

We know that the Old Testament was put into its present shape some-time after the return of Israel from their captivity in Babylon (539 B.C.). That time was a crucial period in the history of Israel. It was a time of severe testing for God's people, a time when Israel's hopes and faith in God's promises had all but been dashed to pieces, a time when it seemed as if those promises were less likely than ever to be fulfilled.

During this time we find Daniel, in captivity in Babylon, pouring over the prophetic books, wondering why God's promises to the fathers had not yet been fulfilled, and seeking the Lord's help in understanding them (Dan. 9:1–2). In his reading of Jeremiah, he had understood that the Messiah and his kingdom would come at the close of the Babylonian captivity. But the end of the captivity had come, and there was still no Messiah.

At that point, God answered Daniel's prayer by sending the angel Gabriel to reveal the precise time of the coming of the Messiah. Gabriel told him that the Messiah would not be coming after the seventy years of exile, as Daniel had supposed from reading Jeremiah (Jer. 25:11). Why? Because, as Daniel's prayer of confession (Dan. 9:4–19) shows, Israel had not remained faithful to God's covenant. They were not ready for the com-ing of the Messiah. His coming would be delayed until their transgres-sion was complete and their wickedness atoned (9:24). That would not hap-pen until after sixty-nine "weeks" of years (9:25–26)—that is, 483 years. Though it is not a simple matter of calculation, the traditional reckoning of years from Daniel's day to the coming of Jesus fits comfortably within that time frame.

The Old Testament Scriptures were thus collected and shaped dur-ing that dark hour of Israel's history. The people were in great need of renewed hope in the promises of God. They were in need of a "more cer-tain" prophetic word, as "a light shining in a dark place" (2 Peter 1:19). Those who gathered and formed the books of the Old Testament into the single collection we now possess were eagerly awaiting the Messiah. They read the Scriptures with that hope in mind, and their expectation is reflected in their work. The shape they gave to the final form of the Old Testament canon was, in effect, a reading sequence that enabled one to see more clearly the picture of the Messiah. It was as if in their arrangement of these texts, they wanted to provide the reader with an appropriate context for understanding and appreciating their messianic message.

Consolidation of the Old Testament

Consolidation is the process by which the Bible adjusts to its environment and its environment adjusts to it. The environment of the Bible consists of the communities within which it was read, preserved, and transmitted. The Old Testament has had two major environments, Judaism and Christianity.

A close relationship has always existed between the Old Testament and Judaism. There would be no Judaism without the Old Testament, and there would be no Old Testament without Judaism. But we know virtually nothing about the process of the completed Bible's taking hold of and shaping early Judaism. What we do have are the results of the merger of the Bible with Judaism etched into the surface of the Bible itself. In many ways, the surface of the Bible is like the surface of the moon, which preserves clear evidence of many collisions with its environment. Also like the surface of the moon, there is a dark side of the Old Testament, showing more signs of collisions than what we see. That dark side is the version of the Hebrew Old Testament that underlies the early translations, such as the Greek and Latin translations (though in some cases, those same translations have also preserved a much smoother, untouched surface than the Hebrew).

What do we mean by "collisions"? A collision between the Old Testament and its environment (e.g., Judaism) consists of points of tension between what the Bible says and what the community would like it to say. The Hebrew Bible, for example, says that the Davidic King, who is to reign over the kingdom of David forever, is none other than "Almighty God" (Isa. 9:6). That thought was apparently too difficult to imagine in the Jewish community that preserved the Masoretic text. Thus that text was accented so that the Davidic King is not called Almighty God, but merely "the Prince of Peace." In the Hebrew text used by the Greek translators, the Davidic King is called simply God's "messenger." In neither community was it conceivable that this person could be divine. Note that those communities did not simply change the text to fit their beliefs. It was far more complex than that. Communities shape texts and texts shape communities. Consolidation is a process that is not clearly understood, but, like the craters on the moon, it leaves clear evidence of having occurred.

The New Testament clearly implies that the Old Testament was also consolidated within early Christian communities. The Isaiah 9 passage, for example, lies behind's Luke's portrayal of Jesus as the Son of God (Luke 1:32).

Hebrew Manuscripts

There are today thousands of Hebrew manuscripts of the Old Testament. Some are ancient; others are brand new. Handwritten copies of the scrolls of the Torah, the first section of the Hebrew Bible, are used every week in Jewish worship services, much like they were in Jesus' day. Such manuscripts are still being copied today. Modern scrolls are made of calfskin parchment. Professional scribes use turkey feather quills and specially prepared black ink. Each day a scribe must rise early in the morning, bathe at a ritual bathhouse, and attend the temple, where he prays and recites the daily reading of texts before going to his work. A scroll of the Torah consists of 5,845 verses, 79,856 words, and 400,945 Hebrew letters. It must be written carefully, one letter at a time. As he writes each letter, a scribe recites a line of text, then the word on which he is working, and then each letter he writes. For him, this process is a religious duty.

Over the centuries, various centers of Judaism have produced their own distinct copies of the Hebrew Bible. The city of Tiberias was a major scribal center during the early Middle Ages. Before the Jews were expelled from Spain in 1492, that country was a major center for the production of Hebrew manuscripts. Other important centers have been Northern Europe, Egypt, Palestine, and Babylon (modern Iraq).

Until a little over two hundred years ago, most of these Hebrew manuscripts remained in the hands of the communities and descendants of those responsible for their production. Some were discarded or lost. In the late eighteenth century, biblical scholars searched out these ancient manuscripts, collected them for study, and put them in major libraries and museums for safekeeping (e.g., the British Museum, the Vatican Library, and the St. Petersburg Library). Those manuscripts are still on display and available for study at those libraries. Many of them have also been reproduced on microfilm and are thus easily available to scholars today.

Ancient Hebrew manuscripts fall into three major groups. (1) The largest portion are Masoretic, the earliest of which were copied between A.D. 600 and 1000. They form the basis for most modern editions of the Hebrew Bible. (2) The Dead Sea Scrolls collection consists of a large collection of very ancient Hebrew manuscripts. (3) An important collection of Hebrew manuscripts of the Torah has been preserved in the non-Jewish communities of the Samaritans.

The Dead Sea Scrolls

In 1947, a shepherd boy looking for a lost goat accidentally came across a cache of ancient manuscripts in a cave near the Dead Sea. The caves were located in the same area as Qumran, an ancient site now in ruins. Thus the scrolls are referred to as the Qumran Scrolls. It was long believed that the community that lived at Qumran was composed of scribes whose lives were devoted to copying biblical manuscripts, which they then stored in the nearby caves. Some archaeologists now doubt whether the caves and the ruin at Qumran are connected in any way. They believe that the ruins at Qumran were originally a private resort of a wealthy Judean.

The manuscripts in the caves were written on leather (parchment) and were stored in ceramic jars. When first discovered, they were sold to a sandal maker, to be used as sandal leather. Fortunately, someone noticed the writing on them, and they were taken to a specialist for appraisal. Thus, by accident, the modern world came into the possession of ancient Hebrew manuscripts that had been preserved unnoticed and untouched for centuries.

The origin of the these scrolls is still shrouded in mystery. Modern dating techniques suggest they were copied from the fifth century B.C. to the first century A.D., mainly in Jerusalem. They were placed in these caves sometime before the Romans destroyed Jerusalem in A.D. 70. Caves further south also contain early manuscripts from a slightly later period (second century). Most manuscripts from the Dead Sea caves had, by the time of their discovery, been reduced to fragments. Some of them, however, have been preserved intact and are in mint condition.

It is difficult to overstate the importance of the Hebrew biblical manuscripts and fragments that have come from this collection. Many fragments have been pieced together and remnants of other manuscripts restored. These represent nearly every book of the Old Testament and give us a glimpse of the form of the Bible that Jesus himself used. We now have a picture of the state of the Hebrew text nearly a thousand years older than was previously available. Among the scrolls is a complete manuscript of Isaiah and a nearly complete copy of Habakkuk. When we compare them with later Hebrew manuscripts, they are virtually identical. The main differences lie in their spelling. The Dead Sea Scrolls have thus demonstrated the remarkable accuracy with which the Old Testament texts were copied and preserved. There are, however, some differences between the present Hebrew text and those at Qumran. These have helped us get a clearer picture of the extent to which later tradition may have affected the Hebrew Bible.

Printed Editions of the Hebrew Bible

With the invention of the printing press, many printed editions of the Hebrew Bible began to appear in the late fifteenth century. The first printed edition (1477) consisted of three hundred copies of the book of Psalms, together with a rabbinical commentary on the text. The manuscripts used for that edition are not known. With few exceptions, the text was printed without the vowel or accent signs. The first edition of the entire Hebrew Bible was printed in 1488; it contained vowel points and accents but no accompanying rabbinical commentary.

An important early edition of the entire Hebrew Bible was printed in 1494, consisting of an earlier printed edition of the Pentateuch, the *Brescia Pentateuch* (1492), and Prophets and the Writings. It was small in size and intended by its editor to be easily carried and read. This was the edition Martin Luther used for his famous German translation of the Bible. It was also used for the Latin translations of Robert Stephanus (1539; 1544–46) and Sebastian Münster (Basel, 1535), two books that were influential in later English translations, such as the King James Version.

The first Christian publication of the printed Hebrew Bible was the *Complutensian Polyglot* (1514–17). A "polyglot" is an edition of the Bible in multiple languages. The one contained the Old Testament in Hebrew, Aramaic, Greek, and Latin. It gets its name from the Spanish city of Alcala, called Complutum by the Romans. Prominent in the center of the page was the standard Latin version, the Vulgate. The Hebrew text was printed along one side of the Latin text and the Greek Old Testament translation along the other side. The Aramaic text, with a Latin translation, was printed across the bottom of the page. In some cases the Hebrew text was altered to suit the Latin translation.

The most important Jewish edition of the Hebrew Bible was that of Daniel Bomberg in 1525, called the *Second Rabbinic Bible*. Its editor, Rabbi Jacob ben Chayyim, a noted biblical scholar, had studied the major Hebrew manuscripts of the Bible in libraries throughout Europe. He was an authority on the traditional Masorah; thus he reproduced the entire Masoretic text of the Hebrew Bible, with vowels, accents, and traditional Masorah. It was the accepted text of the Hebrew Bible for the next four hundred years. In 1937, a new printed edition of the Hebrew Bible came out, the *Biblia Hebraica*, edited by Rudolf Kittel and printed in Germany. It was revised under the title *Biblia Hebraica Stuttgartensia* in 1977. Two new editions of the Hebrew Bible are presently underway: (1) *The Hebrew University Bible*, published in Israel, and (2) *Biblia Hebraica Quinque*, published in Germany.

The Greek New Testament

Greek Writing

The New Testament is written in common Greek, called *Koine*. Greek was the international language of the first century, spoken throughout the ancient world as the language of business and commerce. The Greek of the New Testament was also greatly influenced by the language of the Greek translation of the Old Testament.

About two hundred years before the birth of Christ, the Hebrew Bible was translated into Greek. This translation was called the Septuagint, meaning "the Seventy." It received that name from a popular story that this was the work of seventy scholars from Palestine, commissioned by Egyptian officials to translate the Old Testament for the famed library in Alexandria. Though there may be some truth to the story, in all likelihood it arose as an attempt to lend official recognition to the translation itself. To translate the Word of God into a language other than Hebrew was still a new concept in those days.

The translation was definitely the work of Greek-speaking Jews who lived in Alexandria. They attempted to render the Hebrew text as literally as possible, yet they also wanted it clearly understood in Greek. The result was a Greek version of the Hebrew Bible whose language was greatly influenced by Hebrew. That is the type of Greek we often find in the New Testament. The same phenomenon can be seen in communities that still rely on the King James Version. Often in their speech and prayers one hears the familiar "thee" and "thou" of the King James Version.

The Greek of the New Testament is noted for its precision of expression and wide range of vocabulary. Greek was especially adept at forming compound words. When the apostle Paul, for example, wished to express the unique origin of Scripture and its continued relevance in the life of the Christian, he coined the term *theopneustos*, a word that literally means "God(*theos*)-breathed(*pneustos*)" (2 Tim. 3:16). Though the term had not been used before, it was clear to Greek readers what the term meant: Scripture has a life-giving quality that comes only from God.

The New Testament authors used the full range of expression offered them through the Greek language. The language of the Septuagint also worked to their advantage, for many of the technical terms necessary for the development of Christian theology (e.g., "redemption," "righteousness") had already been developed in that translation. The noun "gospel" and the verb "to evangelize" themselves were borrowed from the Greek Old Testament.

The use of the Greek Old Testament in the New Testament also greatly helped the church to accommodate itself to the teaching of the Old Testament.

Written Records

Some of the data in the New Testament was in written form before being used by the New Testament authors. In the prologue to his Gospel, for example, Luke gives an account of how he came across the materials he used: "Many have undertaken to draw up an account of the things that have been fulfilled among us, just as they were handed down to us by those who from the first were eyewitnesses. . . . Therefore, since I myself have carefully investigated everything from the beginning, it seemed good also to me to write an orderly account for you. . ." (Luke 1:1–3). Luke outlines three stages: (1) the "eyewitness" accounts of the life and sayings of Jesus; (2) those accounts "handed down to us" (middlemen, who wrote down those accounts); and (3) the Gospel writers.

Luke is not clear how the first two stages occurred, but the study of the Gospels suggests that these were written documents. Most New Testament scholars believe an early collection of the sayings of Jesus circulated widely before the Gospels were written, though no such document exists today. It also seems apparent that Jesus himself never wrote anything, nor do we find any indication that his disciples recorded his words and deeds as they traveled. Nevertheless, from the fact that the words of Jesus existed and that they were not contested by the early church, we do know that someone somewhere had written down the events and teachings of Jesus at an early stage.

In books other than the Gospels we find evidence of other types of written records. There are, for example, early "confessions" or creeds of the church. Paul mentions a tradition that he passed on to the Corinthians: "Christ died for our sins according to the Scriptures, . . . he was buried, . . . he was raised on the third day according to the Scriptures" (1 Cor. 15:3–4). Such creeds were probably the centerpiece of early Christian worship. Songs sung in the early church were also an important written source for the New Testament authors (cf. Col. 3:16). Songs are recognizable by their poetic structure, some of which have been preserved in the New Testament (e.g., the hymn about Christ's humility in Phil. 2:6–11). We also find summaries of early Christian teaching. Paul may have drawn from such teaching when he enumerated the "fruit of the Spirit" (Gal. 5:22–23). No doubt his letters contain segments of his own teaching and preaching. Some New Testament writers even made use of other New Testament books (cf. 2 Peter 3:15). There is compelling evidence that both Matthew and Luke used Mark's Gospel.

Book Making

The Egyptians had been making and importing a writing material called papyrus for several thousand years. Papyrus, made of the papyrus plant, was strong and durable and could be used to make scrolls up to twenty-five feet. A papyrus document was often wrapped around a decorated wooden staff, with the writing only on the inside. The scroll was held with the right hand and rolled with the left hand. When not in use it was kept rolled on the right side so that the beginning of the book was exposed. The contents of the scroll were noted at the end where they were most likely to be preserved.

Leather was also used for scrolls. Large leather scrolls were not wrapped around wooden poles, but were held by the leather scroll itself to gain more support. A leather manuscript of Isaiah from the second century B.C. was discovered among the Dead Sea caves. Its leather sides are greatly soiled from the many hands that held it. A leather sheath was sewn to the front to protect it when not in use. It was about twenty-five feet long and sewn together with linen thread.

The Greeks had used papyrus since the seventh century B.C. At the time the New Testament was written, books were written on either papyrus or leather scrolls (cf. Paul's books in 2 Tim. 4:3, which are probably parts of the Hebrew Bible). Jews wrote their Scriptures on the treated skins of ceremonially clean animals.

The original New Testament was undoubtedly written on papyrus or leather scrolls, most likely the former. In the second century, the scroll began to be replaced by the codex. The codex book form was pioneered by the Christian church and only later adopted by the rest of society. The church preferred the form because of its ease of reading and study, for a scroll was more cumbersome to use. The codex was also more portable and thus would be more efficient in travel and in times of persecution.

In a codex, pages of papyrus were cut and bound along one edge, and the pages were written on both sides. All extant copies of the New Testament in the second and third centuries are written on papyrus codices. In many cases, earlier papyrus scrolls were cut and bound into codices. In the fourth century, when the church gained power and wealth, New Testament manuscripts began to be written on finely prepared leather (parchment). The invention of paper was imported from China to Europe in the eleventh century.

Composition of the New Testament

What was said about the composition of Old Testament books holds true for the New Testament, except that there are different book types in the New. The letter, for example, is not known in the Old Testament as an independent book type. The composition of a letter is self-evident. The writer puts his thoughts down on paper, follows a certain formal pattern, signs it, and sends it off to its destination by means of a personal carrier (see especially the book of Philemon). New Testament letters could also be more complex. The books of Luke and Acts, for example, are written as letters, both addressed to Theophilus (probably a Roman official).

The New Testament letters present an interesting insight into the earliest Christian literature. They reveal the inner workings of a small and personal body of believers who had real needs that had to be addressed. These letters offered help to the young churches in the form of exhortation and teaching. Such exhortations and teachings provide a helpful background for understanding the purpose of the Gospels.

Chronologically, the Gospels were written after the letters. They were not directed to individual churches but rather addressed the needs of the church as a whole. As written works they consciously pick up the thread of narrative left off by the last of the Old Testament books (i.e., 1 and 2 Chronicles). The book of Matthew intentionally begins with a genealogical link between Jesus and the genealogies of Chronicles. The author also takes up the theme of Immanuel, "God with us," the final word of promise in the Old Testament (2 Chron. 36:23).

Matthew and John were presumably eyewitnesses to the events they recorded, though they also relied on written records in their versions of the events. Considerable literary dependency exists among Matthew, Mark, and Luke. Most biblical scholars believe that Matthew and Luke used Mark's Gospel in writing their own. Matthew also used written records of the life and teaching of Jesus that Luke apparently did not have. Luke had access to "many" eyewitness accounts of Jesus' ministry (Luke 1:1). The Gospel of John includes much material not in the other three Gospels. Since the Gospels were all written before the end of the first century, not much time had elapsed between the time of Jesus' ministry and their writing.

The last book in the New Testament, the Revelation of John, is apocalyptic literature, the type found in the book of Daniel. It relies almost entirely on prophetic visions.

Redaction of the Gospels

In the New Testament, *redaction* has a different meaning from the Old Testament, where it refers to later additions made to a biblical book. Redaction in the New Testament refers instead to the way in which the Gospels were composed.

When Matthew, Mark, and Luke are compared, it is evident that the authors relied considerably on the same written sources. Though no written records of the supposed sources for the Gospels are known today, the close, almost verbal, similarity of the written material in the three Gospels strongly argues for such written sources.

The basic pattern for the Gospels was established by Mark, and both Matthew and Luke followed his outline. Many believe Mark's Gospel follows the outline of the first sermons preached in the early church. There are, for example, striking similarities between the outline of Mark's Gospel and the sermons of Peter in Acts. That would explain how Mark's Gospel received apostolic authority. This Gospel concentrates on three aspects of the life and ministry of Jesus: (1) his works and miraculous wonders in the regions of Galilee; (2) his journey to Jerusalem to suffer for the sins of humanity; and (3) his death and resurrection in Jerusalem. The whole of Christ's life is portrayed against the backdrop of Old Testament messianic themes.

What sources did Mark use? Here we can only judge from a close analysis of his narrative. Presumably he used small, perhaps independent, accounts of the deeds of Christ. In other words, Mark was the originator of a book-length account of Christ's life. He arranged those early reports into an outline of the events. Those reports were, in all probability, written accounts, though some may have circulated orally as well. The original accounts would have been written in Aramaic, the language of the Galilean Jews at the time of Christ. They had probably been translated into Greek by the time Mark used them. Mark also had access to written records of the teachings of Jesus. Two examples are his parables (Mark 4) and Jesus' teaching about "the last days" and his future return (ch. 13).

Matthew and Luke then used much of what Mark had gathered, adding material from their own particular sources on the teachings of Jesus and on his ministry. Each of the Gospel writers tells the story of Jesus from his own unique perspective. They are not merely retelling the same story, but interpreting the meaning of Jesus for their audience.

The New Testament Canon

To speak of the New Testament canon is to speak of a recognized authority and a specific collection of twenty-seven books. The development of this canon falls into three stages: (1) from the time of the composition of the New Testament books to the middle of the second century; (2) from the middle to the end of the second century; and (3) from the third to the fourth centuries.

(1) The first stage, the time of the apostles and the early church, is known primarily from within the New Testament itself. In Christ's day and during the first years of the church, the only Bible the church had was the Old Testament. Jesus' ministry was punctuated with references to the Hebrew Scriptures (Luke 24:44). The missionary and pastoral activity of the apostles was also guided by and grounded in the Old Testament (Acts 28:23). But already from the beginning of Jesus' ministry, a new canonical authority was making itself heard—the teachings of Christ. Christ spoke with authority (Mark 1:22, 27), and the signs he performed witnessed that he was sent from God. The concept of a New Testament canon was thus already in the air. Jesus himself said to his disciples that the Holy Spirit "will guide you into all truth . . . taking from what is mine and making it known to you" (John 16:13–14). Clearly in these words is the notion of the canonical authority of Jesus' teaching.

In such a context, the Gospels, as the bearers of Jesus' message, were surely recognized as canonical. Moreover, in Peter's lifetime the letters of Paul were already considered as "Scripture" alongside the Old Testament (2 Peter 3:15). Thus very early, the New Testament writings assumed a canonical authority, though there were no official lists of canonical books.

(2) The period from the middle to the end of the second century is marked by much theological division, and the need for an official list of canonical books was beginning to be felt. As the apostles passed from the scene and general Christian literature, some orthodox and some heretical, began to increase, the church was forced to clarify which of its books were authoritative. In this second period, then, canonical lists of New Testament books began to appear. Since these were drawn up to meet specific local needs, none of them was considered comprehensive. Most lists, however, included the four Gospels, the letters of Paul, and some general letters.

(3) By the middle of the fourth century, official and complete lists began to be published. The first official list was issued by the church father Athanasius in 367.

Consolidation of the New Testament

For the Greek New Testament consolidation meant adjustment to various Christian communities that were being formed. The theological, social, and political forces that shaped the church also influenced the formation of their Greek texts. Thus, it was unavoidable that minor changes in the New Testament text would make their way into the manuscripts. As these became standardized and passed on to future generations, textual "families" were formed. A *textual family* is a collection of manuscripts with the same or similar characteristics.

Communities that produced textual families later developed into major centers of the Christian church. In some, the Greek language continued for many centuries; in others, it was replaced by the local vernacular. In the former, the Greek New Testament became deeply rooted in the traditions and practices of the local churches. Where those churches exercised a wide and lasting influence on many others, their particular "family" of manuscripts became the common form of the text throughout that region. In communities where Greek gave way to the vernacular, their Greek families of the New Testament were lost or discarded. When those New Testament manuscripts were found centuries later, scholars realized that they often preserved a form of the Greek New Testament with fewer changes incorporated.

There were at least four major centers of Christianity in the Greek-speaking world: (1) the church of Asia Minor, which later developed into the political and theological center of the Eastern Church, the Byzantine empire; (2) the church in Rome, which became the center of the Western Church; (3) the church in Alexandria, Egypt, which was at one time a major center but which gave way to local dialects; (4) the church in Syria.

From these four major centers, four manuscript "families" developed. The most influential Christian community in the Greek-speaking church was the one in Asia Minor. Copies of the Greek New Testament in Asia Minor were standardized early in the theological school at Antioch. The severe persecutions of Christians in the middle of the third century resulted in the destruction of many New Testament manuscripts. These, of course, had to be replaced, just at a time of great expansion within the church. Official scribal schools thus arose in Asia Minor to meet the need for more manuscripts. The multiplication and spread of their manuscripts meant the spread of the specific manuscript "family." By the medieval period, that "family" of manuscripts, called the Byzantine Text, represented the majority of all New Testament texts and became the basis of all English versions of the New Testament until the late nineteenth century.

New Testament Greek Manuscripts

There are several thousand New Testament Greek manuscripts, most of them now stored in libraries and private collections. Many of them have come to light only in the last century.

The earliest Greek manuscripts, dating from the second and third centuries, were written on papyrus. They were recovered from sites such as the arid regions of Egypt that had dry enough climates to preserve the delicate papyrus material. Unfortunately, the New Testament papyrus manuscripts deposited in moist climates, such as Asia Minor or Greece, have long since succumbed to decay and deterioration. But since the early church was mobile, manuscripts in a certain region may not, in fact, have been copied there. It is thus possible that manuscripts from Asia Minor have been preserved in Egypt. We may suppose, then, that the present collection of New Testament manuscripts is fairly representative of the New Testament in the second century.

The earliest New Testament manuscripts were written on scrolls. But by the middle of the second century, they were being written in codex form. Later on, the church produced large and expensive editions written on treated leather (parchment) and copied by professional scribes, often sponsored by wealthy families. Several of these New Testament codices have been preserved, some dating from as early as the fourth century.

Two such manuscripts are Codex Vaticanus, now kept in the Vatican Library, and Codex Sinaiticus, now kept in the British Museum. These two manuscripts share many similarities with earlier papyrus manuscripts from the second century. Moreover, many early church fathers appear to quote from copies of the New Testament similar to them. Such evidence strongly suggests that these fourth century codices preserve the purest form of the New Testament. They have become the basis for virtually all modern editions of the Greek New Testament.

Ironically, these codices were not highly regarded by the church during most of its history. In fact, they fell into disuse in the Middle Ages. Instead, the church used Greek manuscripts that came from the Byzantine empire. The center of the Greek-speaking Eastern Church was the old city of Byzantium (Constantinople). Because of its wide influence, the Byzantine text family became the "common" text (or the "Majority Text"). After the Byzantium empire fell to Islam in 1453, Christian Greek scholars fled to the West, carrying copies of their Greek New Testament. The Western church was thus flooded with Byzantine copies of the New Testament. When the first printed editions of the Greek New Testament were published, this text was virtually the only form of manuscripts known.

Printed Editions of the Greek New Testament

Printed editions of the Greek New Testament play an important role in the development of the English Bible. The first edition of the Greek New Testament was prepared in Switzerland in 1516 by the learned humanist, Erasmus. This scholar used the manuscripts available to him in the library at Basel, which were primarily late medieval manuscripts of the Byzantine text family. This edition influenced biblical studies and theology for centuries. That text was accepted as the "received text" (*textus receptus*) or the Majority Text and became the text of common usage.

Though Erasmus corrected his text several times, few subsequent biblical scholars ventured to differ greatly from his text. The printed edition of the New Testament by Robert Stephanus in 1550 is a case in point, for his text perpetuated essentially the same *textus receptus* as Erasmus. Stephanus' text became the standard New Testament text in England until the rise of modern critical editions in the late nineteenth century. It had a major influence on early English translations of the Bible, such as the "Authorized Version" (i.e., the "King James Version"). A year later (1551), Stephanus published an edition of the Greek New Testament that included the verse divisions (chapter divisions had been inserted into the Latin Bible by Stephan Langton, Archbishop of Canterbury, about 1205).

As more manuscripts came to light, editors of the Greek New Testament began to weigh the differences between various manuscripts and make minor changes to the *textus receptus*. One of the first New Testament scholars to develop principles of textual criticism to guide such decisions was Johann Albrecht Bengel. His 1734 edition of the Greek New Testament followed the *textus receptus*, but also offered comments and corrections to the text in the margin. Such marginal notes soon became commonplace in printed editions of the New Testament. In this section, called the apparatus, texts that varied from the printed edition of the *textus receptus* were recorded, though the *textus receptus* always remains the base text.

The decisive break with tradition came in the nineteenth and twentieth centuries. Printed editions today provide the reader with a reconstructed Greek text. When manuscripts differ, the editors decide which of the various texts is most likely the original and put that reading in the printed text. Notations of other manuscripts are listed in the apparatus. The *textus receptus* is thus no longer the preferred text. Such texts are called "critical texts," because they provide a text-critically reconstructed text. Most modern translations are based on these critical texts.

Versions of the Bible

Early Versions

In our look at the early versions of the Bible, we are using the term "versions" in a general way. Ordinarily, the term means a translation of the Bible, such as the King James Version or the New International Version. But the notion of a version of the Bible includes the fact that even in the original languages of the Bible we find "versions." There is, for example, a modern Greek version of the New Testament, which enables modern Greek readers to understand the New Testament in their own modern language. Languages change, and readers need to have ancient texts updated, even though they were written in their own language.

In the ancient world, the biblical text was often "updated" and "modernized." This, in effect, amounted to the production of a new "version" of the Bible. Much, in fact, of our present-day Hebrew Bible is written in a form of Hebrew that is more modern than the Hebrew of Moses' day, dating from about the time of the return of the people from the Babylonian captivity (sixth century B.C.). In that sense, the "original" text of the Bible itself appears to have been modernized and updated. The Hebrew language, however, continued to change, and the Jews felt a further need to update their Bible. Copies of the Old Testament were thus written in an updated form of Hebrew and copies of the New Testament in an updated form of Greek.

Discoveries of manuscripts from the Dead Sea Scrolls reveal that at the time of Jesus, there were many such "modern versions" of the Hebrew Bible. Some of them were like modern paraphrases—using new words for outdated ones, rephrasing awkward sentences of the older Hebrew texts, and adding paraphrases to clarify a passage. In general these copies of the Hebrew Bible offered the first-century reader a smoother, easier-to-understand version of the Bible.

Such versions of the Bible in their original language are important for at least two reasons. (1) The New Testament writers often appear to have used such modern versions of the Old Testament when they quoted from the Old Testament. (2) The early translation of the Hebrew Bible into Greek, the Septuagint, also appears to have been based on such versions. Often when the Greek Old Testament renders the Hebrew Bible in an unusual way, lying behind that translation is a "modernized Hebrew version." Moreover, when the New Testament writers used the Greek translation of the Old Testament, they did so because they preferred the Hebrew text underlying it to that of the more ancient text.

Hebrew Versions

A simple example of an early Hebrew version of the Old Testament comes from Deuteronomy 31:1. The original Hebrew reads: "And Moses went and spoke these words to all Israel . . . and he spoke to them. . . ." The phrase "And Moses went" seems awkward. Moreover, why does it repeat the fact that Moses spoke to the people? The NIV, in fact, has smoothed it out with a paraphrase of its own: "Then Moses went out and spoke these words. . . ." Even here, though, the difficulty remains. Where did Moses go? Why did he go somewhere before he spoke? Though this is not a major issue, the original Hebrew text reads awkwardly here.

A fragment of the text of Deuteronomy found among the Dead Sea Scrolls has resolved the difficulty. There the text reads smoothly: "Now when Moses had finished speaking to all Israel, he said. . . ." This makes sense within the larger view of the book—Moses has just finished the speeches he began in Deuteronomy 1:5, and now he speaks his last words to Israel. How did the Hebrew scribe achieve his solution? The Hebrew words "he went" and "he finished" have the same four consonants: WYKL. The original text has WYKL, which means, "he went"; the Hebrew paraphrase has WYLK, which means, "he finished." All the scribe had to do to smooth out his text was to exchange the last two letters: KL—> LK. Early interpreters commonly tried to make sense of a difficult passage by switching the letters. Incidentally, the Septuagint of Deuteronomy is identical to the fragment from the Dead Sea Scrolls.

A similar example can be seen in the Septuagint of the difficult Hebrew expression in Habakkuk 2:4, "his desires are not upright." The Greek translator rendered this, "My soul takes no pleasure in him." In the Hebrew text this "version" amounts to little more than the exchange of two letters. Since the difference is related to the Hebrew text, it is likely that the Greek translator used a Hebrew text that was, in fact, a paraphrase of the difficult original Hebrew expression. In this way, the Septuagint serves as a witness to an early paraphrastic Hebrew version of Habakkuk. What makes this example particularly interesting is that this passage is quoted in Hebrews 10:38, where the author uses Habakkuk 2:4 to encourage Christians not to shrink back from trusting God and thus be destroyed. He quotes this verse from the Septuagint and from the early Hebrew version of Habakkuk that underlies it.

Greek Versions

We have just seen that the early Greek versions of the Old Testament preserved earlier Hebrew versions and paraphrases of the Old Testament. The Greek versions are thus translations that help in understanding the text of the Old Testament. We have thousands of early Greek manuscripts of the Old Testament, most of them representing the Septuagint. Strictly speaking, the Septuagint is the early Greek translation of the Hebrew Pentateuch. In more general usage, however, the term has come to be used for the earliest Greek translation of the entire Old Testament. We know little about its origin; much of that is clouded in legend. We do know, however, that one or two centuries before Christ, Greek-speaking Jews made the bold venture of rendering their sacred Hebrew Scriptures into the language of the Gentile world.

Their efforts met with such success that few translators attempted to duplicate their work. The early church and many of the New Testament writers relied heavily on this version. Likewise the Jews who lived in the Greek-speaking world used it as their accepted and somewhat official version of the Bible. In time, however, there was a parting of ways. The Greek-speaking church held on to the Septuagint as its own Bible, but the Jews abandoned it in the second century and began a lengthy process of replacing it. Greek-speaking Jews still needed a Greek translation of the Hebrew Bible, of course, but were unwilling to use the Septuagint. They replaced it with several revised versions of the Septuagint. The three most important of those versions are known by the names of their editors or revisers: Aquila, Symmachus, and Theodotion.

Why did the Jews abandon the Septuagint? There are two, not unrelated, answers. (1) As already suggested, throughout the first century Jews made wide use of various updated versions of the Hebrew Bible. At the close of that century, however—perhaps because of the destruction of the temple in Jerusalem or the growing presence of Christianity, who also relied on the Old Testament—Jews, driven from their homeland, united around a single version of the Hebrew Bible, the version that was later to become the Masoretic text. Since the Septuagint represented a version of the Bible dissimilar to the version they retained, from their perspective they could no longer accept it. (2) The Septuagint had been translated during a period when many Jews were awaiting the fulfillment of the Old Testament messianic promises. The Septuagint often reflected that hope and thus was of great use to Christians, who believed Jesus was that fulfillment. In debates with Christians, Jews preferred a version of the Bible that reflected their current understanding of the text.

The Septuagint

The Septuagint is the most important Greek translation of the Old Testament, reflecting the meaning of the Hebrew Bible held by ancient Jews throughout the Greek-speaking world. The translation was already completed by the time of Jesus, and many New Testament writers relied heavily on it. The Septuagint appears to have used a version of the Hebrew Bible slightly different than our present Hebrew text. It is thus an important window to the past.

To translate the Hebrew Bible into Greek was a formidable task for several reasons: (1) Hebrew and Greek are such different languages; (2) the Old Testament is so enormous; and (3) nearly every Hebrew word required deliberate choices by the translators about the meaning and interpretation of the Bible. The Greek translators were covering new ground. Never before had the Scriptures been translated into any language. What word, for example, should be used to render the Hebrew word for "God"? What word should be used for "law"? The choices they made would directly affect how the revelation of God in the Hebrew Bible would be understood not only by Greek-speaking Jews, but by all Greek-speaking people. Their choice of words and expressions became the basic vocabulary of the New Testament and Christianity.

In their translations, however, their interest was much more focused on the needs of the hour. When they translated the Mosaic law, for example, they used the word *nomos*, a word that referred to the statutes and regulations by which an orderly Greek city was governed. In giving the law, therefore, Moses was cast in the Septuagint as the founder of the Israelite state. When they rendered the description of the land in Genesis 1:2 as "an unformed mass," they laid the ground rules for all future discussions of the meaning of creation.

Moreover, the translators clearly read their Hebrew Bible as a prophecy. They believed that the Messiah would be born of a virgin, for they choose the specific Greek word *parthenos* ("virgin") to render the prophetic promise in Isaiah 7:14. They also believed that David's psalms were written as prophecies of the coming Messiah, and they labeled them as written "for the end [days]" (from the superscription to Psalms), that is, the days of the coming Messiah. When Peter, in his sermon on Pentecost, quoted from Psalm 16 to prove that the Messiah would rise from the dead, he quoted from the Septuagint (Acts 2:25–26), reflecting a different tradition from the Hebrew text we now have. Peter's point would have been harder to establish from that text.

Post-Septuagint Jewish Greek Translations

Because of the overwhelming popularity of the Septuagint among the early Christians and because it did not fully represent the official Jewish Hebrew Bible, Jewish scholars in the second and third centuries began "correcting" their Greek Bibles. That process resulted in several new Greek translations. The best known of these was Aquila's, a second-century Roman citizen who converted first to Christianity and then to Judaism. Only fragments of his translation exist today, though the nature and purpose of the work is not difficult to assess. It was designed for Jews who wanted to know what their newly standardized Hebrew text meant in Greek.

Aquila did not start over from scratch; rather, he revised the Septuagint. Where it translated a different Hebrew text than the one now accepted, he inserted his own translation. Where the Septuagint interpreted the Hebrew Bible differently than in his day, he again provided his own interpretation. Aquila's straightforward style has earned him the reputation of being a literalistic translator. However, a literalistic translation can be a means of avoiding an alternative meaning for the text, and we can only guess at his motives. Why, for example, did he translate Genesis 1:1 "in the head" rather than "In the beginning"? True, the Hebrew word for "beginning" comes from the same root as "head," but it also means "firstborn." Does Aquila want to give a new sense to this text, or does he want to hide an old one? We know that much Jewish-Christian debate in the Middle Ages centered on the meaning of the word "beginning" in Genesis 1:1 and how it might apply to Jesus as the "firstborn over all creation" (Col. 1:15). If that debate had already begun in the second century, then Aquila's translation played a role in that debate.

The same can be said for his notorious translation of the Hebrew direct object particle. In Hebrew, the direct object of a verb is marked by a word that can also be understood as the preposition "with." Aquila, for some unknown reason, always translates this particle with the Greek word for "with," even when it makes little sense. Thus he renders Genesis 1:1 as "God created with the heaven and with the earth." Since this part of the verse was also a point of contention between Jews and Christians, Aquila could have wanted to neutralize the Christian interpretation. In Isaiah 7:14, where the Septuagint uses *parthenos* ("virgin"), Aquila uses the Greek word *neanis* for "young maiden," thus ruling out the Christian proof for the virgin birth.

Aquila was not the only early Greek reviser of the Septuagint. In the late second century, two Jewish-Christian biblical scholars, Symmachus and Theodotion, each produced a revision of the Septuagint in the Greek of their day. Little is known of either translation today.

The Hexapla

By the beginning of the third century, the Old Testament had assumed various forms. A standardized Hebrew version was the accepted text of Judaism. The Greek Old Testament existed as the Septuagint and its three primary revisions—Aquila, Symmachus, and Theodotion.

Much of the early apologetic task of the church centered on the church's claim that the gospel was grounded in the message of the Old Testament. That claim was disputed both by the pagan world and by Jews. Unfortunately, few Christian apologists were well versed in the intricacies of the Hebrew language, which had only consonants and required arduous training to read. In any event, most Christian apologists and their opponents accepted the basic ground rules that the debate could proceed from the Greek text. But it was important to know the extent to which the Hebrew text differed from the Septuagint. A tool was thus needed to allow Greek readers to peer behind their translations and see what was, in fact, in the Hebrew text. To that end the great biblical scholar Origen set out to compile his Hexapla.

The word "Hexapla" means "six columns." It was a multi-language edition of the Old Testament, arranged word for word in parallel columns. On the left side of the page, Origen wrote the Hebrew word. That was followed by a transliteration of the word, with vowels, into Greek, to show how it was pronounced. The third column was the Greek word used by Aquila in his translation; the fourth, fifth, and sixth columns gave the translations of Symmachus, the Septuagint, and Theodotion respectively.

In the Hexapla, the fifth column was the most important, for it contained the venerated Septuagint. To show how it differed or agreed with the Hebrew text, Origen marked the words of the Septuagint with "minus" marks to show words not in the Hebrew text. And when the Hebrew text had words not translated in the Septuagint, Origen added Greek words from one of the other translations and marked them as additions. This work was thus a important document in the early history of the Bible. It was too lengthy to be copied and thus was kept in Caesarea, where it was compiled. It remained there for several centuries; when it was destroyed, it could not be replaced.

The copy of the Septuagint in the Hexapla was so respected that virtually all subsequent copies of the Greek Bible were made from its fifth column. Unfortunately, many copies were made without Origen's notations of additions and minuses.

Greek Versions of the New Testament

Just as there were various Hebrew versions of the Old Testament in the first century, so there also developed several distinct versions of the Greek New Testament, called "families" (see the above unit, "Consolidation of the New Testament"). The two most important families of Greek manuscripts were those which developed in the eastern half of the Roman empire and those that developed in Egypt. Evidence for the family of manuscripts in the western empire is primarily preserved in Latin translation.

The differences among the textual families of the Greek New Testament manuscripts are, for the most part, not major. Each family has its unique characteristics. The Byzantium text, for example, is noted for its tendency to gather variants from other textual families and add them to its text. In other words, it tried to be all things to all people. The Alexandrian text (i.e., the family of manuscripts from Egypt), on the other hand, was more conservative. It was either unaware of other families or unconcerned about them. In any event, it appears to have persisted the longest without significant change. For that reason most modern editions of the Greek New Testament rely heavily on that group of manuscripts.

There is one example of what appears to be a genuine Greek paraphrase of the New Testament. That form of the New Testament text is now represented in a large codex, called Codex D, copied in the late fifth century. Though few specifics are known about its author, he was apparently an important theologian in his day. He read the New Testament text closely, especially Luke and Acts, and was concerned that his readers might miss important aspects of the stories. He thus inserted explanations and added information to tie the whole together. In the story of the conversion of the Philippian jailer in Acts 16:25–40, for example, the additions reveal his close attention to detail. In the earliest Greek text of Acts, there seems to be no direct connection between the magistrates' releasing Paul and Silas and the earthquake that destroyed their jail. In Codex D, however, the writer has inserted the comment that the magistrates released Paul and Silas "because they remembered the earthquake and were afraid." The purpose of a paraphrase is not to change the meaning of the text, but to clarify it by making it more explicit. The fact that this manuscript is written in two columns, one in Greek and the other in Latin, suggests it was used within a church setting, perhaps for public instruction. It is, in any case, a valuable witness to attitudes about the Greek New Testament at this early stage.

The Latin Versions

As Christianity spread throughout the Roman empire, the common people needed translations in their language. In the first two centuries, Greek continued to be spoken in the large centers of the Roman empire, including Rome. But in outlying regions (e.g., North Africa), Latin was the principal language. Early translations of the Bible into Latin began to appear. These early translations were made from the Septuagint and from a text family of the New Testament known as the "Western Text." For several centuries these early Latin versions enjoyed wide circulation.

The spread of these versions, however, was largely uncontrolled. By the fourth century, the need was felt for a more unified text as a basis for formulating doctrine and church practice. The pope thus commissioned the biblical scholar Jerome, a linguist and Hebrew scholar, to produce a single, unified Latin edition of the Bible. Though deeply influenced by the Septuagint, Jerome translated the entire Hebrew Old Testament into Latin, completing it in 405. For the New Testament, Jerome relied heavily on the existing Latin versions. His translation was not accepted universally in the Latin church, but in time it replaced all others. It became the "common" Bible of the medieval church in the West—hence its title, the Vulgate ("common Bible").

The major reason for its popularity was, of course, that it was written in good Latin. By the time of the Reformation, however, there were other reasons for its wide recognition. In response to the Reformers, the Catholic Church attempted to demonstrate that its claims were based on the truths of Scripture. Since many of those claims were based on the Vulgate, the Catholic Church argued that it was to be taken as the authoritative text. The Council of Trent (1546) asserted (1) the equal validity of Scripture and Tradition as sources of religious truth, (2) the sole right of the church to interpret the Bible, and (3) the authority of the text of the Vulgate.

At several points, the doctrines of the Catholic Church rested exclusively on the Vulgate. (1) In Genesis 3:15, for example, the Vulgate translated the Hebrew "He will crush your head," as "She will crush your head," making Mary the ultimate victor over Satan. (2) In Genesis 14:18, Melchizedek is said to have "sacrificed" bread and wine and was thus a model for the priesthood. (3) Genesis 6:5b mitigated the idea of original sin. While the Hebrew text made the human heart "only and always set on evil," the Vulgate rendered the human heart as merely "prone to evil."

(4) The future tense of the verb in John 14:26 suggested that the Holy Spirit "*will* reveal whatever [Jesus] *will* say" to his church, rather than what Christ *did say* to them (past tense). This was used to show that the later decrees of church councils were to be accepted as oracles of the Holy Spirit.

Aramaic Versions

During the time of the Persian empire, the common language was Aramaic. Israelites taken into Babylon had learned to speak Aramaic, and that language eventually replaced Hebrew as their mother tongue. Dialects of Aramaic continued to be spoken in Syria and Northern Palestine at the time of Christ. The native language of Jesus was most likely a dialect of Aramaic.

In most early synagogue services, the Hebrew Scriptures were read a verse at a time and then translated into Aramaic. No doubt they were even translated into written Aramaic, though few copies of such translations remain. Parts of the Old Testament itself were written in Aramaic (e.g., Dan. 2:4–7:28). Many of the written sources for the Gospels were most likely in Aramaic. Since this language is similar to Hebrew, it became a sort of second language of the Bible.

The earliest Aramaic versions of the Old Testament took the form of commentary and explanation rather than mere translation. They were by and large written for bilingual communities who understood both Hebrew and Aramaic. Thus, they were designed to help a Jew understand the meaning of the Scriptures. Such Aramaic translations were known as "Targums" (Aramaic word for "translation").

The Targums performed an immensely important function for the Hebrew Bible, for they preserved the meaning of the Hebrew language and words. In the course of time, Hebrew ceased to be a living language among Jews. But the Targums preserved the meaning and sense of the Hebrew into the medieval period. When Jews again began seriously to study biblical Hebrew in the Masoretic period, there were no longer living speakers of the language. To restore knowledge of Hebrew, Jews turned to the Targums, where they found the original meanings of the Hebrew words and sentence structure intact. Even obscure idioms were preserved.

The Targums also preserve early Jewish interpretations of the Old Testament. Messianic interpretations, for example, abound, reflecting the beliefs of Jews before the rise of the Masoretic text. Some Targumic interpretations date back to the first century. Targums also provide many parallels to interpretations of the Old Testament found in the New.

Another common Aramaic language in the early Eastern Church was Syriac. Though its exact origin is unknown, the Syriac version of the Bible was widely read and highly influential during most of the history of the Eastern Church. That version, known as the *Peshitta* (meaning "the simple or common" version), is an excellent translation. It relies extensively on the Septuagint and the early Targums.

English Versions

The origin of the English Bible is linked to four key historical events: (1) the spread of Christianity into the British Isles, (2) the development of the English language, (3) the continuing role of Latin as the language of the church, and (4) the rapid decline of the influence of the Roman Catholic Church in Britain in the fifteenth century.

(1) Acts describes the spread of Christianity from Jerusalem to Rome in the first century. During this time, the Roman empire was conquering Britain. As Christianity spread, it inevitably found its way into Britain. By the seventh century, it was well established there and began to grow under the monks schooled in the Christian culture of the empire. The center of their activity was a monastery at Canterbury. The language of learning was Latin, not the native Anglo-Saxon.

(2) English as a language began in the fifth century when the Germanic tribes of the Jutes, Anglos, and Saxons conquered the Celtic tribes of Britain. By the middle of the seventh century, Caedmon, an early Christian poet, had composed extensive biblical paraphrases in Anglo-Saxon, which had a lasting influence on English translations. In the eighth century, an Anglo-Saxon version of Psalms and a translation of the Gospel of John were produced in Britain. In the ninth century, King Alfred provided a translation of the Ten Commandments and parts of Exodus as a prologue to his collection of laws. In the tenth century, the four Gospels, the Pentateuch, Joshua, Judges, Esther, and parts of other books were translated into Anglo-Saxon.

(3) The basis of these translations was the Vulgate. When the French-speaking Normans invaded Britain in 1066, Anglo-Saxon merged with French to form the first stage of modern English. Because Latin continued as the language of learning and study of Scripture, there was little encouragement from the church to translate the Bible into English.

(4) As the Roman church declined in Britain in the late fifteenth century, more serious efforts to translate the Bible into English began. The first effort was John Wycliffe's translation of the New Testament (1380). This was followed by a partial translation of the Old Testament done by Nicholas de Hereford, which Wycliffe himself completed. The entire translation was revised by John Purvey after Wycliffe's death. Since it was nearly a century before the invention of printing, all of their work was published in manuscript form only, though Wycliffe's translation and Purvey's

revision were widely circulated. The invention of the printing press and the flourishing of English literature in the sixteenth and seventeenth centuries aided the development of modern English. William Tyndale's translation of the New Testament signaled a new era of the English Bible.

The Rebirth of Learning

By the mid–1400s the intellectual and spiritual life of Europe began to be fundamentally transformed (the period known as the Renaissance, meaning "rebirth"). In the fifth century, the great classical cultures of Greece and Rome had fallen prey to invading Germanic tribes; culture and learning survived only in the cloistered halls of secluded monasteries, where monks studied Latin and copied Latin translations of the Bible. Outside Europe, however, classical learning was still being preserved in the Eastern empire. The study of New Testament Greek was highly cultivated in Constantinople throughout the medieval period, and the knowledge of biblical Hebrew survived in Spain and the Near East. Not until the late Middle Ages, however, did the Western church benefit from such learning. Several factors led to the rebirth of learning.

(1) An important starting point was the publication of literary works in the language of the people. In the early fourteenth century, for example, the Italian poet Dante published his *Divine Comedy* in Italian. Many men of letters followed that example, including the English poet Chaucer, who published *Canterbury Tales*.

(2) Another factor was a growing desire to get behind the Latin translations of the great works of the past (including the Scriptures) to the original texts. Scholars also wanted to translate the classics into the language of the common people. One thing that distinguished Luther from other priests in his day was his attention to the study of Greek and Hebrew.

(3) In 1453 the Muslim Ottoman Empire captured Constantinople and ended the Greek-speaking Eastern empire. Many Greek scholars fled to the West, bringing with them New Testament Greek manuscripts and the skills to read and study them. A short time later, Jewish scholars, who had flourished in the great centers of Judaism in Spain, began a forced exile into Europe and the Near East, bringing along many manuscripts and skills in Hebrew. They eagerly shared those skills with Christians who wanted to read the Hebrew Old Testament.

The convergence of these factors with the invention of the printing press in Europe meant an unprecedented opportunity for growth in biblical learning and translation in the English world. One of the first biblical scholars to take full advantage of these factors was William Tyndale.

William Tyndale

With the English translation of the Bible by William Tyndale (1524–33), the history of the English Bible took a decidedly new turn. He was the first one to render an English version directly from Hebrew and Greek. Tyndale's own education in the classics at Oxford and Cambridge uniquely equipped him for work in the field of ancient languages. His generation was the first generation of biblical scholars to have a full line of scholarly tools available.

As Tyndale began his translation of the New Testament, he used the new edition of the Greek New Testament by Erasmus. And when he began translating the Old Testament, the new and definitive edition of the Hebrew Bible had just been printed by Jacob ben Chayyim. It was natural, and indeed providential, that Tyndale took on the task of translating the Bible anew.

Tyndale had a lifelong commitment to the idea that Scripture should be rendered in the language of the common people. Before beginning his work, he carefully thought through the problems such a translation would entail and developed specific principles to aid in achieving his goal. Those principles set the standard for all subsequent English translations. He was convinced that a translation of the Bible should come from the personal study of the Scriptures by the translator, not from the legacy of previous translations. He thus paid little attention either to earlier English versions of the Bible or to versions in other languages. He was influenced by the Latin Vulgate, of course, as well as Luther's German translation, but he was not slavishly dependent on them.

It is easy to miss the importance of the role Tyndale played in making the modern English Bible. He established the basic vocabulary, style, and thought forms of all future English translations. Most readers today are familiar with the "meaning" of the English Bible through classical translations, such as the King James Version, or modern translations, such as the New International Version. Those versions are the legacy of William Tyndale. They have preserved and passed on the essential shape and meaning he gave the biblical text.

English translations are not simply the natural consequence of casting the meaning of Greek or Hebrew words into the grammar and idioms of the English language. There are any number of ways to render a text into English. The specific choice of words, the proper rhythm and tone, the level of formality—these are all essential features of a translation that must be determined by the translator. The singularity of style, tone, and focus that is common to most modern versions reflect the influence of Tyndale's own personality on the English text.

From Tyndale to the King James Version

In England during the fifteenth and early sixteenth century, translating the Bible into the English vernacular was forbidden (William Tyndale himself did his work in Europe). It was even forbidden to possess or use an English translation. Ostensibly, medieval church authorities were afraid that the uneducated laypeople would fall victim to erroneous beliefs if left to study the Scriptures on their own, though there was also power in possessing the only access to Scripture.

The Reformation of the sixteenth century, however, was also felt in England. In 1534 a convocation of English church leaders gathered at Canterbury to petition the king, Henry VIII, to allow the publication of an English Bible. Tyndale's translation of the New Testament and parts of the Old Testament were already in circulation, but penalties were stiff for those caught reading them. Though the king gave no official response, in the next year, he allowed the Coverdale Bible to be published. This Bible was less objectionable to church authorities because it relied on the official Vulgate and did not contain critical marginal annotations, as Tyndale's had. Though a learned Greek scholar, Miles Coverdale did not know Hebrew.

Taking advantage of the new climate of toleration, John Rogers, a Protestant and a friend of Tyndale, republished much of Tyndale's translation, adding several sections of previously unpublished Old Testament sections and supplying the rest from Coverdale's Bible (1537). This edition, called "Matthew's Bible," became the basis for several English revisions that ended in the King James Bible. Rogers included notations considered inflammatory by some church officials. Thus, a new edition of Matthew's Bible was commissioned, the task being assigned to Coverdale. The result was the "Great Bible" (1539). In that edition, Coverdale relied heavily on the superb translation and annotations of the German scholar and linguist Sebastian Münster. Thus in the Great Bible, Tyndale's English Bible survived and obtained a new level of competence that represented the best of European biblical scholarship at that time.

Continental scholarship was to play an even greater role in the formation of the English Bible in the years ahead. During Mary's reign in England, many Protestant biblical scholars fled to Geneva, where William Whittingham continued the task of revising the English Bible. He began with a revision of the New Testament (1557) and completed the entire Bible in 1560. That edition was the "Geneva Bible." It was the most popular English Bible for the next fifty years, though the Great Bible continued as the official English Bible. The Bishops' Bible (1568) was a revision of the Great Bible. The Douay-Reims Bible (1610) was a translation of the Vulgate.

Biblical Studies in the Sixteenth and Seventeenth Centuries

The foundation on which the Protestant Reformation was built was *sola Scriptura*—that is, "Scripture alone." The Scriptures alone are the Word of God, the final judge in all matters of faith and practice. To know them is to know God's will. The meaning of Scripture lies in its literal sense; there are no hidden levels of meaning beyond that sense. Needless to say, such a starting point led to an immense surge in biblical scholarship. This was felt first in the advances in the systematic study of Greek and Hebrew.

In order to understand Hebrew, Christians at first relied on Jewish sources. During the Middle Ages, Jewish scholars developed a thorough analysis of biblical Hebrew and the Hebrew Bible. Lexicons were meticulously prepared, grammars written, and the Hebrew text submitted to an almost inexhaustible examination of its details. Most of this knowledge about the Bible was stored in compressed biblical commentaries of famous rabbis (the most famous was Rabbi Solomon ben Isaac, known to Jewish scholars as Rashi). Jewish editions of the Hebrew Bible were known as "rabbinic Bibles," because along with the Hebrew text, the commentaries of the great rabbis were printed. Each page consisted of a portion of the biblical text, its corresponding portion in the Aramaic Targum, and the relevant rabbinical commentary. Most of the comments explained the "simple" or "plain" meaning of the Bible.

The most important edition of the Hebrew Bible in the sixteenth and seventeenth century was ben Chayyim's edition of 1525, a rabbinic Bible. It was published for Jewish scholars by the Christian printer, Daniel Bomberg. Christian biblical scholars were well acquainted with these rabbinical commentaries, lexicons, and grammars, and used them as the basis of their own Hebrew studies and understanding of the Old Testament.

The result of the burst of energy that went into the study of the original languages of Scripture was a series of learned translations of the Bible. These translations were written by scholars and for scholars, and thus they were written in Latin. Accompanying these translations were copious annotations and commentaries on every aspect of the text. Christians, in other words, began to mimic the rabbinic Bibles. By the time of the Geneva Bible and the King James Version, therefore, translators had numerous helps available to them.

The King James Version (1611)

When Queen Elizabeth I died and James I succeeded her to the English throne, England had two versions of the Bible: the Bishops' Bible and the Geneva Bible. Anxious to preserve the unity of the church, the king wasted no time in commissioning a new "authorized" translation. According to the plan the king himself drew up, forty-seven translators were assigned specific portions of the Bible. They were divided into three panels: Panel 1 met at Westminster, assigned Genesis through 2 Kings and Romans through Jude; Panel 2 met at Cambridge, assigned 1 Chronicles through Ecclesiastes and the Apocrypha; Panel 3 met at Oxford, assigned Isaiah through Malachi and the Gospels, Acts, and Revelation.

Well represented among the translators were the professors of biblical Hebrew and Greek from both Oxford and Cambridge. These men represented the highest caliber of biblical and theological scholarship in the English world.

The plan of the translation given to the three panels called for a revision of the Bishops' Bible, "to be followed, and as little altered as the truth of the original will permit." The translators were each to take the same section of text and, separately, make their own revisions. They were then to meet together to compare their revisions and settle on a common result. As each of the three panels completed a single book, their results were to be sent to the other two for their evaluation and consideration. If one of the panels took issue with the work of the other, it was to send notification of its disagreement to them. If a difference remained among the panels, it would be resolved by a meeting of the key members of each panel.

As can be seen, King James was not seeking a new translation so much as standardizing existing versions. An additional panel was to be convened to examine the final product and make suggestions with regard to current usage in English and the appropriateness of the theological terms. The translators worked for almost three years. Their overall task was to make a good translation (the Bishops' Bible) into a better one (the King James Version).

After the King James Version was begun, publication of the Bishops' Bible ceased, though it was many years before the new version supplanted the Geneva Bible in private use. Nevertheless, with the publication of this Authorized Version (as it is sometimes called), the work of providing an English version of the Bible came to a conclusion. Not until the late nineteenth century did interest in a new version of the English Bible surface again.

The Rise of Biblical Criticism (*Critica Sacra*)

An important chapter in the history of the Bible is the rise of biblical criticism. Biblical scholars in the seventeenth century realized that the task of studying and maintaining the ancient biblical documents required an increasing expertise. Major universities in England and Europe established special departments and research positions to foster the "critical" study of Scripture. Orthodox biblical scholars insisted that the church had a right and a duty to apply "critical" analysis to the biblical text, so long as that entailed a humble submission to its authority. They understood the word "critical" to mean "analytical." One applied "criticism" to the Bible, for example, when one removed a scribal addition to a biblical manuscript and restored it to its original state, or when one uncovered a lost meaning to an ancient Hebrew word.

In this sense, the application of "criticism" to the Bible was no different than to any other ancient document. Languages change over time, and manuscripts suffer mistakes and oversights when copied. Special care and attention must be given to biblical manuscripts. To ensure that such tasks were carried out in the spirit of humility and doctrinal fidelity, biblical scholars called for a special discipline, a *critica sacra* ("sacred criticism"). Under its terms they were allowed to submit the Bible to close scrutiny, but were never to allow themselves to become masters over the Bible itself. The Bible they investigated always remained the sacred Word of God.

"Sacred criticism" resulted in many advances in biblical studies during the seventeenth and early eighteenth centuries. Massive biblical commentaries and great tomes on the history of the manuscripts were produced. One of the unfortunate drawbacks of the period, however, was the optimistic evaluation of the Hebrew manuscripts representing the Masoretic text. Most biblical scholars and theologians vehemently maintained that the Masoretic texts, including the vowels signs and accents, were exact replicas of the "autographs" and that they were inspired in all those details. In taking such a position, they were set up for a fall in the ensuing years. As long as the biblical texts were given the benefit of the doubt, as was the case with "sacred criticism," these scholars could insist that their manuscripts represented the originals. With the introduction of a new kind of criticism, however, the benefit of the doubt was removed. When that happened, doubt was to become an essential feature.

The Rise of Biblical Criticism (*Critica Profana*)

With an increasing number of biblical scholars in the late seventeenth and eighteenth centuries, a new attitude towards the Bible began to emerge. Put simply, the Bible came to be viewed solely as a document from a past era and was thus accountable to the same kind of impartial criticism as any other ancient document. Whereas many scholars were arguing for the *critica sacra*, others were beginning to argue for more objectivity. They wanted a *critica profana* ("common criticism"), which treated the Bible the same as other ancient documents.

There is a subtle, but real, difference between these two attitudes. The objective of "sacred criticism" was a close scrutiny of the biblical manuscripts, in order to purge them of such things as scribal errors and later additions and to present to the reader the "original text." The objective of "common criticism," however, was to submit a judgment or evaluation of the "original text" itself, in order to rid the biblical text itself of ideas and attitudes that were deemed antiquated and thus unworthy of serious consideration. The Bible began to be regarded as a product of an earlier, more primitive age. The task of biblical scholarship was to sift through the Bible and evaluate what remained valid and true and what should be discarded.

In the late seventeenth century, a few biblical scholars began expressing these ideas. Throughout the eighteenth century, however, biblical scholarship began to define itself in terms of *critica profana*. The turning point that led from a "sacred criticism" to a "common" one was part of a larger change in attitude throughout European society. Society's view of God and the world, for example, began to change. Many rejected outright the notion of divine providence. They held that the universe was guided by its own internal and universal laws and that God's will was not a direct factor in its operation. Moreover, they rejected the idea of special revelation. God had not broken into the web of causes and effects to order to express his will directly to human beings. Thus, there was no longer any certainty that the course of God's acts in history were adequately reflected in the actions recorded in Scripture. At best, the Bible merely recorded human religious responses to God's presence in the world. In the minds of these scholars, the link between history and the description of history in the Bible could no longer be sustained.

The Rise of Biblical Criticism
(Historical Critical Method)

The move from a *critica profana* to "historical criticism" was a small and natural step. Once biblical scholars accepted that God works only through natural processes and the normal course of historical events, they were free to act as if the Bible could be approached through those processes and events. There was no longer any need for the supernatural. Thus the Bible could be studied and scrutinized solely as a part of the regular course of human history. That method became known as "historical criticism" or the "historical critical method." It reached its full development by the beginning of the nineteenth century and continues to govern many modern approaches to Scripture.

The historical critical method has a twofold purpose. (1) It attempts to reconstruct the most natural explanation for the origin and development of the Bible. What, for example, are the historical processes that led to the writing and preservation of the Old and New Testaments? The explanations given within the Bible itself are not necessarily valid. According to such critics, phenomena like miracles and fulfilled prophecy are not valid categories for explaining the Bible and the historical events recorded in it. (2) It attempts to explain the origin and development of the people who gave us the Bible. It looks to sources other than Scripture to determine the history of Israel and the early church. Here too, the historical critical method rules out miracles and divine providence in its explanations.

Throughout its growth and development, the historical critical method encountered intense opposition. Classical Jewish scholars opposed it because it threw into question the validity of the Bible's claim to tell the true history of Israel. Classical Christian orthodoxy also opposed it because it limited the meaning of Scripture. Even a casual reading of the Bible indicates that its writers believed in a God who works miracles in this world and that true prophecy is possible. A method designed to rule out those two fundamental principles is surely too narrow to explain the Bible adequately.

Modern evangelical approaches to Scripture have characteristically followed the line of classical orthodoxy and *critica sacra*. Evangelicalism starts with the divine gift of the gospel and the promise of eternal life—things grounded in biblical concepts such as divine providence and miracles. Evangelicalism thus rejects the basic tenets of the historical critical method.

The Eclipse of the Bible

Before the rise of historical criticism in the seventeenth and eighteenth centuries, the Bible was read literally and historically as a true and accurate account of God's acts in history. The realism of the biblical narratives indicated that the biblical authors described historical events exactly as they had happened. Moreover, the real world was identified as the world described in the Bible, and one's own world was meaningful only insofar as it could be viewed as part of the world of the Bible. The concept of divine providence was essential to holding together the depiction of events in the biblical narratives and the occurrence of those events in history. God was the author of both the Bible and the events that the Bible depicts.

The medieval theologian Thomas Aquinas gave a definitive expression of this idea: "The author of Scripture is God, in whose power it is not only to use words for making known his will (which any human being is able to do), but also historical events in the real world." For this church scholar, the course of human events was a real story written by God in the real world. "History" is "his story." Such a reading of the biblical narratives is "precritical," since it reflects an attitude of taking the Bible at face value and reading it as it was originally intended. The key element in this view of the Bible and history is divine providence.

Over the last two centuries, this precritical understanding of Scripture has been gradually eroded by an increasingly historical reading of the Bible. We have grown accustomed to looking for biblical meaning beyond the narratives themselves. The aim of biblical interpretation has begun focusing on the process of reconstructing "what really happened" in the historical events. The meaning of the Bible was not what the Bible depicts but what historians come to believe really happened as they apply the tools of historical research. Therefore, biblical scholars pay less attention to the text and devote most of their attention to reconstructing historical events.

The loss of such a link between devotion to Scripture and the study of the biblical text means that the task of describing the relationship between God's acts in history and the record of those acts in Scripture has passed into the domain of historical science. Whereas previously one could turn to Scriptural exegesis to learn about God's acts in history, now one must resort to a scientific and historical reconstruction of the events. For many, history rather than Scripture has thus become the focus for understanding the Bible's meaning.

Biblical Studies in the Nineteenth and Twentieth Centuries

The scholarly study of the Bible focused on historical research in the nineteenth century. Advances in a historical understanding of the Bible continued in the twentieth century, but with a new awareness of the role that hermeneutics, the science of interpretation, plays in understanding the past.

Progress of historical studies of the Bible in the nineteenth century centered in the sciences of philology and archaeology. (1) Philology is the study of ancient texts. It includes the analysis of early manuscripts and the description of the ancient languages of those manuscripts. The nineteenth century saw significant discoveries of Old and New Testament manuscripts. (a) The two most important New Testament manuscripts "discovered" were Codex Sinaiticus and Codex Vaticanus. Neither had been lost, but both had laid in out-of-the-way places, unnoticed and unappreciated for centuries. These two manuscripts have now become the basis for all modern editions of the New Testament, beginning with the Revised Version of 1881. (b) With financial assistance from the Czar of Russia, two large collections of Hebrew manuscripts were gathered and cataloged in the great library of St. Petersburg. The manuscript that now serves as the basis of the modern edition of the Hebrew Bible was "discovered" among them. (c) In the nineteenth century for the first time, scholars deciphered ancient inscriptions of the Egyptians and Babylonians. These languages shed much light on the language and history of the Bible.

(2) The science of archaeology came into its own in the nineteenth century. Though its techniques left much to be desired, archaeology made great strides toward filling in many "unknowns" of ancient Near Eastern history. Many artifacts and texts now on display in the great museums of the world were gathered and cataloged during this century. Many "discoveries" of the twentieth century were actually made in basements of those large European libraries, where materials were brought but never unpacked. A version of the Babylonian account of the flood resembling that of the Bible was "discovered" while being cataloged for the British Museum.

The twentieth century has seen an unprecedented surge in our knowledge of the Bible and of the ancient Near East. So great is the importance of that material that we are including an entire volume on this topic in the *Zondervan Quick-Reference Library*. With the abundance of that information comes the task of sorting and interpreting it so that it becomes meaningful in relationship to the Bible. The twentieth century thus has focused on the issue of interpretation.

The Revised Version (1881–1885)

The King James Version of the Bible had been so successful that it remained the standard English version for the next 250 years. Its English was updated and minor corrections inserted, but the general public was content with that version. The New Testament of this version, as we saw earlier, had been translated from the *textus receptus*, that is, the "received text" that grew out of the Eastern Church in the Middle Ages. But biblical scholars now felt that a new English version was justified, with manuscript discoveries of the New Testament that were much older and purer and with work beginning on a new edition of the Greek New Testament.

One must understand that when scholars talk about "inferior" texts, they do not mean worthless or even faulty. They have in mind incidental differences among manuscripts. What scholars especially noticed were many textual additions in the New Testament of the King James Version that were not in the older manuscripts. In other words, nothing of the New Testament was lost in those manuscripts. Rather, scribal additions were included. Biblical scholars in the late nineteenth century wanted, for good reason, to rid the text of such later additions. The manuscripts and text of the Old Testament used in the Revised Version did not differ from those of the King James Version; it was the ben Chayyim text of the Bomberg Rabbinic Bible of 1525.

When the Revised Version of the New Testament appeared in 1881, the work was not widely appreciated by the general public and the clergy. They had little understanding of the reasons behind the changes in the New Testament text. The common argument was based on the role of God's providence in preserving his Word. Why would God allow his church to rely on an "inferior" manuscript family for nearly 1500 years? Does not the fact that the church has used the *textus receptus* for so many years suggest that it is the text God intended for his church?

At the heart of this argument lay the same issues the church had faced in the Reformation, where the Catholic church argued that one thousand years of the Vulgate was sufficient to demonstrate its reliability. The Reformers and the early translators of the English Bible argued that translations should be based on the best texts available—precisely what the translators of the Revised Version were saying.

Another reason for the poor reception of the Revised Version was its policy of rendering many Greek words in a needlessly wooden sense. Each Greek New Testament word was always rendered by the same English word. Though that might put the English reader in closer touch with the original language, it left little opportunity for breadth of expression.

The English Bible in the Twentieth Century

The twentieth century has witnessed an explosion in Bible translations—the aftershocks of the Revised Version's failure to fill a void. Throughout the first half of the century, the King James Version held its own. The Revised Version, though accepted in principle, was never fully accepted in practice. In 1901 a group of American scholars published their own edition of that version, calling it the American Standard Version. Though it enjoyed only marginal success, it became the basis of two important revisions, the Revised Standard Version (1952) and the New American Standard Bible (1971). Each of these revisions acknowledged its dependence on the tradition of English translations that runs from Tyndale to the King James Versions. These two are not new translations, but rather attempts to preserve what was good and useful in light of contemporary English usage and scholarship. These revisions used the latest editions of the Greek and Hebrew texts and the most recent lexical and grammatical studies. In the RSV, for the first time, many alterations based on the Septuagint were made in the Old Testament.

There were also significant theological overtones in the publication of the RSV and the NASB. In the liberal-fundamentalists debates of the first part of this century, a leading issue became the question of the "virgin birth" of Christ. Broadly speaking, liberalism denied the virgin birth, while fundamentalists avidly affirmed it. By the mid–twentieth century, those debates had cooled, but the issue simmered below the surface. With the RSV of Isaiah, this question again rose to the surface, because it reversed a long-standing practice by translating the word *almah* in Isaiah 7:14 by "young woman," rather than "virgin." The NASB was published ten years later with the word "virgin" again intact and with a far more dependency on the Masoretic text. The New International Version followed suit. It is hardly accidental that the idea for the NIV also began to percolate at about the same time.

Thus three major English Bible translations in twentieth-century America grew out of the same stirrings that were never laid to rest in the publication of the Revised Version in the late nineteenth century. To show that the ground has still not settled, the King James Bible itself has been reissued under the title "The New King James Version" (1982). Its editors explicitly state that one of its purposes is to perpetuate the textual tradition begun by William Tyndale and continued by the King James Version.

The English Bible Today

The last two decades have witnessed a virtual explosion of publications of new versions of the English Bible. The most popular English versions today are the NIV (New International Version), the NKJV (New King James Version), NASB (New American Standard Version), and the NRSV (New Revised Standard Version). Each of these is published in a wide variety of formats. There are Bibles for beginners, youth Bibles, study Bibles, devotional Bibles, large print Bibles, Bibles for "boomers," picture Bibles, and so on. A visit to the local Christian bookstore can present a bewildering, but exciting, array of choices for reading the Scriptures.

In actual fact, the choices are not as diverse as one might at first suspect. The English Bible comes to us today in a form that is remarkably homogeneous, regardless of what version one may use. Amid all the diversity lies a fundamental unity. They are all virtually the same "version" of the standard English Bible that has lasted for nearly a half of a millennium.

What accounts for such a uniformity? Though all modern English Bibles make the claim to be "new translations" of the Hebrew and Greek texts, they are, in actual fact, essentially "revisions" of earlier English versions. As our survey of the history of the English Bible has shown, much of what was accomplished by Wycliffe and Tyndale remains today in the "latest" English versions. There are two reasons for this. (1) The basic tools of Bible translation have remained the same during most of the history of the English versions. There have been, to be sure, new discoveries and new tools that shed new light on the meaning of the Hebrew and Greek words and texts, but many of those meanings have not withstood the test of time and have thus not found a secure place within most contemporary English versions. Time has demonstrated the essential trustworthiness of the earlier English versions.

(2) The long-standing English versions have had a profound influence on Christian thought and experience. The church of the English-speaking world is grounded in the traditional English Bible. Theology, worship, and Christian living is defined by our English Bibles. That is not an easy legacy to shed by means of a completely new translation, nor would the church be wise in attempting to shed it. For the average Christian, a change in the English text is tantamount to a change in Scripture itself. There must be solid reasons for a change. English versions that have, in fact, deviated sharply from the common "legacy" of the English versions (e.g., The New English Bible, 1971), have found little acceptance among Christian readers.

Translation Theory and Dynamic Equivalency

The task of Bible translation has changed over the years, even though the essential content of English versions has not. There are essentially two philosophies of translation: literal translation and dynamic equivalent translation. A literal translation attempts to render the Hebrew or Greek original text in a "word for word" manner. Each Greek or Hebrew word is rendered by a corresponding English word. In a dynamic equivalency approach, the words are not so much translated as are the thoughts expressed by the original. The translator asks, "What was the biblical writer saying in his use of these words?" and then expresses this concept in an English sentence. Both literal and dynamic equivalent translations may understand the underlying text in the same way, but they can differ markedly in the way they render the passage. In many cases, a dynamic equivalent translation will express more clearly the thought of a biblical writer than a literal translation.

Let's take an example. The King James Version (1611) rendered Romans 1:17, "For therein (the gospel) is the righteousness of God revealed." The phrase "righteousness of God" is a word-for-word translation of the Greek words Paul used. But in rendering the phrase "literally," what is not conveyed fully is Paul's actual meaning in using the phrase. Does he mean that in the gospel God reveals himself as righteous? Or does he mean that in the gospel believers are made righteous with God? In the New Living Bible, a dynamic equivalency translation, Paul's meaning, at least as it was understood by the translators, is made clear: "This Good News tells us how God makes us right in his sight." What is important to note is that the "sense" of the verse in the New Living Bible is the same as how the King James translators understood it, and basically the same as how the verse has been understood since the time of the King James Version. But the "literal" rendering of the Greek phrase in the King James Version was simply unable to express that meaning as clearly as modern dynamic equivalency translations.

Another feature that often disguises the underlying uniformity of modern English Bibles is the simple fact that the English language, like all other languages, changes over time. The English language has changed so drastically over the last four hundred years that most modern English readers would be unable to read or understand a passage from the original King James Version. The language of that version, as we have noted, was continually, and unofficially, updated throughout the centuries. Nevertheless, it is essentially the same version.

Bible Translation and "Inclusive Language" (I)

It is widely recognized today that with regard to the use of gender, the English language is in the midst of a radical transformation, one whose outcome has yet to be decided. There are powerful and significant influences on today's English. Some are arguing that the English language has been a tool in the past for maintaining a male-dominated culture. The predominant use of such words as "man" as a generic expression for all of humanity, and the use of masculine pronouns such as "he" to express both male and female persons, are interpreted as social mechanisms for male dominance. In actual fact, as in most languages, such masculine forms were always understood as "gender neutral" until recent times, when new meanings were read into these masculine forms.

Regardless of whether male domination was ever the intent behind these features of the English language, a growing sensitivity is now widely recognized, and many in the English-speaking world are striving to obtain a new kind of "gender neutral" language—one that avoids the specific use of masculine forms. Masculine pronouns such as "he" and "his" have been narrowly defined simply as masculine pronouns and are used sparingly, often along with feminine pronouns such as "she" when both male and female are intended.

A person may object to such efforts to change the English language, but the fact remains that the language has begun to shift. Few, even of those who resent the shift, will not admit that the pronoun "he" now has a predominantly masculine meaning. Whereas only a decade or two ago the pronoun "he" was understood as "gender neutral," it no longer has that meaning. "He" means primarily a male person. If one wants to be clearly understood to refer to both male and female persons, one must resort to the use of the "he or she" or the use of the plural "they."

This change in the English language has had an impact on Bible translations. Just as in the everyday use of the English language, the word "man" in the English Bible once clearly referred to both "male and female" (cf. Gen. 1:27 in KJV, RSV, NIV). Today, however, in order to render the "generic" sense more clearly in this verse, the NRSV translates this Hebrew word with "humankind," while New Living Bible renders it as "people."

If such a change in the English language holds, it will certainly affect future English versions now under preparation. Bible publishers have entered into public debate with translators and biblical scholars over the wisdom of following the changes in the English language too closely, or of not following them at all. Just how far can the Bible's meaning be made to conform to the new standards of a changing language, and to what extent are the translators of the Bible also to accept their role in shaping that language? When, for example, John 14:23, "Jesus answered him, 'If a man loves me, he will keep my word, and my Father will love him, and we will come to him and make our home with him'" (RSV) is rendered with "gender neutral" plurals, "Those who love me will keep my word, and my Father will love them and we will come to them and make our home with them" (NRSV), the natural question is whether a change in meaning has also taken place. The use of plurals here gives the sense of God's dwelling with the community of believers, in contrast to the singulars in the original text, which imply God's presence specifically with individuals. Many today are warning the reading public that the demand to keep up with the changes in language may lead to significant changes the meaning of the text.

Bible Translation and "Inclusive Language" (II)

Where this question of inclusive language may prove to have its most serious consequences is in the Bible's references to God. With the loss of the "gender neutral" pronoun "he," the English translators no longer have a grammatically and theologically correct way to refer to God without thinking of God as a masculine. Yet to use the pronoun "she" for God would suggest that God is feminine. Biblically and theologically speaking, God does not have a gender. "He" is neither a "male" nor a "female." The use of the pronoun "he" in reference to God has never meant that the Bible or the church believed that God was a male. God is a person, but a unique person who does not have a gender.

Though that has been the teaching of both the Bible and Christian theology, there appears presently to be no "correct" way to render such a notion into the English language. Several modern English translations follow the practice of continuing to use the "gender neutral" pronoun "he" when it refers to God or when the context supports a clearly masculine person. Elsewhere, other are advocating the use of the new "gender neutral" pronoun "they." Still others are even suggesting the creation of a new gender neutral English pronoun, "s/he."

But such inconsistency in translation surely cannot be a lasting, or even a wise, solution. A basic and unavoidable principle of language is its economy. A language simply cannot long support the use of two distinct forms to express an identical idea. One of the two forms must give way. There is little doubt that if the English language continues to shift away from the standard "gender neutral" expressions, such as "he" or "man," those forms will be increasingly understood as referring purely to masculine persons. If and when then happens, the English Bibles will be put into the strange and seemingly contradictory position of teaching both that "God is not a man" (Num. 23:19) and that we must use only masculine pronouns to refer to him.

In light of the present dilemma, some have argued that Bible translations should assume a more active role in preserving the older "gender neutral" use of masculine forms such as "he," attempting both to stem the tide of the change in English and thus to preserve a vital element of the English language for future Bible readers. It is too early at this point to predict where this debate will end up.

Glossary

Autographs

See section entitled "The 'Original Text,'" p. 21

Babylonian Captivity

See The Exile

The Canon of Scripture

See section entitled "The Canon of Scripture, " p. 11

Codex

The codex replaced the scroll and was the precursor of the modern book. Pages of papyrus or leather were cut and bound along one edge, and the pages were written on both sides.

The Dead Sea Scrolls

See section entitled "The Dead Sea Scrolls," p. 44

The Exile

The exile was a historical event in the life of the people of Israel, in which their country and cities were destroyed and they were taken captive into Babylon (this happened in the sixth century B.C.). This was more than a mere historical event, however, for it also meant that God, who had endured centuries of rebellion on the part of his chosen people, was finally bringing about the due penalty for Israel's sin. God is a just God— a God of mercy and a God of wrath. His mercy was shown in his long delay of sending Israel into captivity; his justice in the destruction of the nation by the Babylonians. The exile was of central importance to the biblical writers, for the Lord himself had become Israel's enemy. The people, who had for many centuries assumed that God would never destroy his own people, now faced the horrible reality that they were living in a foreign land and were captive to a foreign people. Moreover, their own land lay in ruins. *See also* The Return from Captivity

Family (Textual)

A textual "family" is a collection of manuscripts with the same or similar characteristics.

The Majority Text

See section entitled "The Majority Text of the New Testament," pp. 25–26

The Masoretic Text

See section entitled "The Masoretic Text of the Old Testament," p. 22

Messiah, Messianic

Throughout the Bible is a recurring theme of fall and redemption. God created the world good. But his world and its creatures rebelled and now stand in opposition to him. In God's grace, he promised to send a Redeemer—an individual who would defeat the forces of evil and establish a righteous kingdom. This Redeemer is the Messiah, "the Anointed One," who would rule God's creation and all humanity. In the Old Testament he is identified as a king from the tribe of Judah or the house of David, a prophet like Moses, a priest like Melchizedek, or the "Son of Man" who will return in the clouds of the heavens to establish his universal kingdom. In the New Testament the Messiah/Redeemer is Jesus. The term *messianic* is used to describe any and all biblical passages that speak of a future redemption in light of an individual Redeemer.

Mosaic Covenant

Exodus 19–24

On several occasions throughout Israel's early history, God established, and renewed, a covenant between himself and his people. The central passages recounting that covenant are Exodus 19 and 24. In that covenant God promised Israel that they would be a great and wise nation if they would obey him and keep his commandments. Though Israel often transgressed the Mosaic covenant, as in the case of the Golden Calf (Ex. 32), God forgave them and continued his covenant relationship with them. Eventually Israel's rebellion caught up with them, however. The Mosaic covenant had stipulated (Deut. 4:26–27; 28:15–68) that if Israel failed to obey God's law, they would be carried away in exile from the Promised Land. That happened in the Babylonian captivity (*see* The Exile).

The Original Text

See section entitled "The 'Original Text,'" p. 21

Pentateuch

See The Torah

Qumran

See section entitled "The Dead Sea Scrolls," p. 44

The Return from Captivity

The Babylonian captivity was a central event in the life of God's people (*see* The Exile). It meant that God's people were themselves experiencing God's wrath. But the biblical writers also stressed that God's wrath against his own people would not last forever. God, who had allowed his people to be taken to Babylon, would also bring them out of captivity and back into the Promised Land. This return was a central focus of the hope that the prophets put before the people. The prophet Jeremiah, for example, foresaw that the Babylonian exile would last only seventy years, after which God's people would return to the land; this happened when King Cyrus of Persia issued an edict that allowed all who desired to return to the Promised Land. Though there was great hope that the return from Babylon might mean the fulfillment of the messianic hopes of the people, that did not happen. The coming of the Messiah was projected into a much more distant future (see Dan. 9:24–27).

Septuagint

See the sections entitled "Greek Writing," "Greek Versions," and "The Septuagint," pp. 48, 60, and 61

Text Family

See Family (Textual)

Textus Receptus

The printed edition of the New Testament text edited by Erasmus in 1516, representing the Majority Text *(see sections entitled* "The Majority Text of the New Testament" and "Printed Editions of the Greek New Testament," pp. 25–26 and 56). The term also refers to any New Testament text that resembles Erasmus' text.

The Torah

The Torah, the first section of the Old Testament, is made up of five parts. These parts—Genesis, Exodus, Leviticus, Numbers, and Deuteronomy—are usually considered individual books in their own right. In reality, they are merely five segments of the larger work called the *Pentateuch* (a Greek word meaning "five-part book"). The Hebrew word *Torah* means "instruction." The Torah is the foundational document of both the Old and New Testaments. In it the central themes of the Bible are laid down and given their initial development. The subsequent books of the Bible develop these themes in a variety of ways.

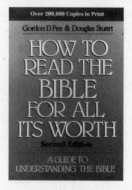
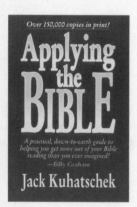